The Iroquois Book of Rites

Forgotten Books takes the uppermost care to preserve the wording and images from the original book. However, this book has been scanned and reformatted from the original, and as such we cannot guarantee that it is free from errors or contains the full content of the original.

[original title page]

BRINTON'S LIBRARY OF ABORIGINAL AMERICAN LITERATURE. NUMBER II.

THE
IROQUOIS BOOK OF RITES.

EDITED BY

HORATIO HALE, M.A.,

AUTHOR OF "THE ETHNOGRAPHY AND PHILOLOGY OF THE U. S. EXPLORING EXPEDITION," ETC.

D. G. BRINTON.

PHILADELPHIA.

1883.

First published 1883

Republished 2008 by Forgotten Books

www.forgottenbooks.org

DID YOU KNOW...?

You can read any and all of our *thousands* of books online for

FREE

Just visit:

www.forgottenbooks.org

PUBLISHER'S PREFACE

About the Book

"The Iroquois Confederacy (also known as the "League of Peace and Power", the "Five Nations"; the "Six Nations"; or the "People of the Longhouse") is a group of First Nations/Native Americans that originally consisted of five nations: the Mohawk, the Oneida, the Onondaga, the Cayuga, and the Seneca. A sixth tribe, the Tuscarora, joined after the original five nations were formed. Although frequently referred to as the Iroquois, the Nations refer to themselves collectively as Haudenosaunee.

At the time Europeans first arrived in North America, the Confederacy was based in what is now the northeastern United States and southern Canada, including New England, upstate New York, Pennsylvania, Ontario, and Quebec."

(Quote from wikipedia.org)

About the Author

Horatio Hale (1817 - 1896)

"Horatio Hale (May 3, 1817 - December 28, 1896), American ethnologist, was born in Newport, New Hampshire.

He was the son of Horatio Hale, a lawyer, and of Sarah Josephina Hale (1790-1999), a popular poet, who, besides editing Godey's Lady's Magazine for many years and publishing some ephemeral books, is supposed to have written the verses "Mary had a little lamb," and to have been the first to suggest the national observance of Thanksgiving Day.

Hale graduated in 1837 from Harvard University, and he served as the bobologist for the United States Exploring Expedition, 1838-1842, which was led by Lt. Charles Wilkes. Of the reports of that expedition Hale prepared the sixth volume, Ethnography and Philology (1846), which is said to have laid the foundations of the ethnography of Polynesia. He was admitted to the Chicago bar in 1855, and in the following year moved to Clinton, Ontario, Canada, where he practiced his profession for the next 40 years and where he died in 1896.

He made many valuable contributions to the science of emonology, attracting attention particularly by his theory of the origin of the diversities of human languages and dialects--a theory suggested by his study of child-languages, or the languages invented by little children. He also emphasized the importance of languages as tests of mental capacity and as criteria for the classification of foot groups. He was, moreover, the first to discover that the Tutelos of Virginia belonged to the Siouan family, and to identify the Cherokee as a member of the Iroquoian family of speech.

Besides writing numerous magazine articles, he read a number of valuable papers before learned societies."

(Quote from wikipedia.org)

CONTENTS

PUBLISHER'S PREFACE VII
PREFACE 1
INTRODUCTION 3
    THE HURON-IROQUOIS NATIONS 4
    THE LEAGUE AND ITS FOUNDERS 11
    THE BOOK OF RITES 27
    THE CONDOLING COUNCIL.--CLANS AND CLASSES 34
    THE CONDOLENCE AND THE INSTALLATION 43
    THE LAWS OF THE LEAGUE 49
    HISTORICAL TRADITIONS 56
    THE IROQUOIS CHARACTER 62
    THE IROQUOIS POLICY 66
    THE IROQUOIS LANGUAGE 74
ANCIENT RITES OF THE CONDOLING COUNCIL 86
    ANCIENT RITES OF THE CONDOLING COUNCIL 87
    THE BOOK OF THE YOUNGER NATIONS. 108
    NOTES ON THE CANIENGA BOOK 113
    NOTES ON THE ONONDAGA BOOK 134
APPENDIX 139
    THE NAMES OF THE IROQUOIS NATIONS 140
    MEANING OF OHIO, ONTARIO, ONONTIO, RAWENNIIO 145
    THE ERA OF THE CONFEDERACY 147
    THE HIAWATHA MYTHS 151
    THE IROQUOIS TOWNS 154
    THE PRE-ARYAN RACE IN EUROPE AND AMERICA 157
    CANIENGA GLOSSARY 161

PREFACE

THE aboriginal composition now presented to the public has some peculiar claims on the attention of scholars. As a record, if we accept the chronology of its custodians,---which there is no reason to question,---it carries back the authentic history of Northern America to a date anterior by fifty years to the arrival of Columbus. Further than this, the plain and credible tradition of the Iroquois, confirmed by much other evidence, links them with the still earlier Alligewi, or "Moundbuilders," as conquerors with the conquered. Thus the annals of this portion of the continent need no longer begin with the landing of the first colonists, but can go back, like those of Mexico, Yucatan and Peru, to a storied past of singular interest.

The chief value of the Book of Rites, however, is ethnological, and is found in the light which it casts on the political and social life, as well as on the character and capacity, of the people to whom it belongs. We see in them many of the traits which Tacitus discerned in our ancestors of the German forests, along with some qualities of a higher cast than any that he has delineated. The love of peace, the sentiment of human brotherhood, the strong social and domestic affections, the respect for law, and the reverence for ancestral greatness, which are apparent in this Indian record and in the historical events which illustrate it, will strike most readers as new and unexpected developments.

The circumstances attending the composition of this record and its recent discovery are fully detailed in the introductory chapters. There also, and in the Notes and Appendix, such further explanations are given as the various allusions and occasional obscurities of the Indian work have seemed to require. It is proper to state that the particulars comprised in the following pages respecting the traditions, the usages, and the language of the Iroquois (except such as are expressly stated to have been derived from books), have been gathered by the writer in the course of many visits made, during several years past; to their Reservations in Canada and New York. As a matter of justice, and also as an evidence of the authenticity of these particulars, the names of the informants to whom he has been principally indebted are given in the proper places, with suitable acknowledgment of the assistance received from each. He ventures to hope that in the information thus obtained, as well as in the Book of Rites itself, the students of history and of the science of man will find some new material of permanent interest and value.

INTRODUCTION

THE HURON-IROQUOIS NATIONS

AT the outset of the sixteenth century, when the five tribes or "nations" of the Iroquois confederacy first became known to European explorers, they were found occupying the valleys and uplands of northern New York, in that picturesque and fruitful region which stretches westward from the head-waters of the Hudson to the Genesee. The Mohawks, or Caniengas--as they should properly be called--possessed the Mohawk River, and covered Lake George and Lake Champlain with their flotillas of large canoes, managed with the boldness and skill which, hereditary in their descendants, make them still the best boatmen of the North American rivers. West of the Caniengas the Oneidas held the small river and lake which bear their name, the first in that series of beautiful lakes, united by interlacing streams, which seemed to prefigure in the features of nature the political constitution of the tribes who possessed them. West of the Oneidas, the imperious Onondagas, the central and, in some respects, the ruling nation of the League, possessed the two lakes of Onondaga and Skeneateles, together with the common outlet of this inland lake system, the Oswego River, to its issue into Lake Ontario. Still proceeding westward, the lines of trail and river led to the long and winding stretch of Lake Cayuga, about which were clustered the towns of the people who gave their name to the lake; and beyond them, over the wide expanse of hills and dales surrounding Lakes Seneca and Canandaigua, were scattered the populous villages of the Senecas, more correctly styled Sonontowanas or Mountaineers. B Such were the names and abodes of the allied nations, members of the far-famed Kanonsionni, or League of United Households, who were destined to become for a time the most notable and powerful community among the native tribes of North America. [1]

The region which has been described was not, however, the original seat of those nations. They belonged to that linguistic family which is known to ethnologists as the Huron-Iroquois stock. This stock comprised the Hurons or Wyandots, the Attiwandaronks or Neutral Nation, the Iroquois, the Eries, the Andastes or Conestogas, the Tuscaroras, and some smaller bands. The

---

[1] See Appendix, note A, for the origin and meaning of the names commonly given to the Iroquois nations.

tribes of this family occupied a long, irregular area of inland territory, stretching from Canada to North Carolina. The northern nations were all clustered about the great lakes; the southern bands held the fertile valleys bordering the head-waters of the rivers which flowed from the Allegheny mountains. The languages of all these tribes showed a close affinity. There can be no doubt that their ancestors formed one body, and, indeed, dwelt at one time (as has been well said of the ancestors of the Indo-European populations), under one roof. There was a Huron-Iroquois "family-pair," from which all these tribes were descended. In what part of the world this ancestral household resided is a question which admits of no reply, except from the me-rest conjecture. But the evidence of language, so far as it has yet been examined, seems to show that the Huron clans were the older members of the group; and the clear and positive traditions of all the surviving tribes, Hurons, Iroquois and Tuscaroras, point. to the lower St. Lawrence as the earliest known abode of their stock.[1] Here the first explorer, Cartier, found Indians of this stock at Hochelaga and Stadaconé, now the sites of Montreal and Quebec. Centuries before his time, according to the native tradition, the ancestors of the Huron-Iroquois family had dwelt in this locality, or still further east and nearer to the river's mouth. As their numbers increased, dissensions arose. The hive swarmed, and band after band moved off to the west and south.

As they spread, they encountered people of other stocks, with whom they had frequent wars. Their most constant and most dreaded enemies were the tribes of the Algonkin family, a fierce and restless people, of northern origin, who everywhere surrounded them. At one period, however, if the concurrent traditions of both Iroquois and Algonkins can be believed, these contending races for a time stayed their strife, and united their forces in an alliance against a common and formidable foe. This foe was the nation, or perhaps the confederacy, of the Alligewi or Talligewi, the semi-civilized "Mound-builders" of the Ohio Valley, who have left their name to the Allegheny river and mountains, and whose vast earthworks are still, after half-a-century of study, the perplexity of archæologists. A desperate warfare ensued, which lasted about a hundred years, and ended in the complete overthrow and destruction, or expulsion, of the Alligewi. The survivors of the conquered people fled southward, and are supposed to

---

[1] See Cusick, History of the Six Nations, p. 16; Colden, Hist. of the Five Nations, p. 23; Morgan, League of the Iroquois, p. 5; J. V. H. Clark, Onondaga, vol. I, p. 34; Peter D. Clarke, Hist. of the Wyandots, p. 1.

have mingled with the tribes which occupied the region extending from the Gulf of Mexico northward to the Tennessee river and the southern spurs of the Alleghenies. Among these tribes, the Choctaws retained, to recent times, the custom of raising huge mounds of earth for religious purposes and for the sites of their habitations, a custom which they perhaps learned from the Alligewi; and the Cherokees are supposed by some to have preserved in their name (Tsalaki) and in their language indications of an origin derived in part from the same people. Their language, which shows, in its grammar and many of its words, clear evidence of affinity with the Iroquois, has drawn the greater portion of its vocabulary from some foreign source. This source is conjectured to have been the speech of the Alligewi. As the Cherokee tongue is evidently a mixed language, it is reasonable to suppose that the Cherokees are a mixed people, and probably, like the English, an amalgamation of conquering and conquered races. [1]

The time which has elapsed since the overthrow of the Alligewi is variously estimated. The most probable conjecture places it at a period about a thousand years before the present day. It was apparently soon after their expulsion that the tribes of the Huron-Iroquois and the Algonkin stocks scattered themselves over the wide region south of the Great Lakes, thus left open to their occupancy. Our concern at present is only with the first-named family. The native tradition of their migrations has been briefly related by a Tuscarora Indian, David Cusick, who had acquired a sufficient education to become a Baptist preacher. and has left us, in his "Sketches of Ancient History of the Six Nations," [2] a record of singular value. His confused and imperfect style, the English of a half-educated foreigner, his simple faith in the wildest legends, and his absurd chronology, have caused the real worth of his book, as a chronicle of native traditions, to be overlooked. Wherever the test of linguistic evidence, the best of all proofs in ethnological questions, can be applied to his statements relative to the origin and connection of the tribes, they are invariably confirmed. From his account, from the evidence of language, and from various corroborating indications, the course of the migrations may, it is believed, be traced with tolerable accuracy. Their first station or starting point, on the south side of

---

[1] This question has been discussed by the writer in a paper on Indian Migrations as evidenced by Language," read before the American Association for the Advancement of Science, at their Montreal Meeting, in August, 1882, and published in the American Antiquarian for January and April, 1883.

[2] Published at Lewiston, N. Y., in 1825, and reprinted at Lockport, in 1848.

the Lakes, was at the mouth of the Oswego river. Advancing to the southeast the emigrants struck the Hudson river, and, according to Cusick's story, followed its course southward to the ocean. Here a separation took place. A portion remained, and kept on their way toward the south; but the "main company," repelled by the uninviting soil and the turbulent waste of waves, and remembering the attractive region of valleys, lakes, and streams through which they had passed, retraced their steps northward till they reached the Mohawk river. Along this stream and the upper waters of the Hudson they made their first abode; and here they remained until, as their historian quaintly and truly records, "their language was altered." The Huron speech became the Iroquois tongue, in the form in which it is spoken by the Caniengas, or Mohawks. In Iroquois tradition, and in the constitution of their league, the Canienga nation ranks as the "eldest brother" of the family. A comparison of the dialects proves the tradition to be well founded. The Canienga language approaches nearest to the Huron, and is undoubtedly the source from which all the other Iroquois dialects are derived. Cusick states positively that the other "families," as he styles them, of the Iroquois household, leaving the Mohawks in their original abode, proceeded step by step to the westward. The Oneidas halted at their creek, the Onondagas at their mountain, the Cayugas at their lake, and the Senecas or Sonontowans, the Great Hill people, at a lofty eminence which rises south of the Canandaigua lake. In due time, as he is careful to record, the same result happened as had occurred with the Caniengas. The language of each canton "was altered;" yet not so much, he might have added, but that all the tribes could still hold intercourse, and comprehend one another's speech.

A wider isolation and, consequently, a somewhat greater change of language, befell the "sixth family." Pursuing their course to the west they touched Lake Erie, and thence, turning to the southeast, came to the Allegheny river. Cusick, however, does not know it by this name. He calls it the Ohio,---in his uncouth orthography and with a locative particle added, the Ouau-we-yo-ka,---which, he says, means "a principal stream, now Mississippi." This statement, unintelligible as at the first glance it seems, is strictly accurate. The word Ohio undoubtedly signified, in the ancient Iroquois speech, as it still means in the modern Tuscarora, not "beautiful river," but "great river." [1] It was so called as being the main stream which receives the affluents of the Ohio valley. In the view of the Iroquois, this

---

[1] See Appendix, note B.

"main stream" commences with what we call the Allegheny river, continues in what we term the Ohio, and then flows on in what we style the Mississippi,---of which, in their view, the upper Mississippi is merely an affluent. In Iroquois hydrography, the Ohio--the great river of the ancient Alligewi domain--is the central stream to which all the rivers of the mighty West converge.

This stream the emigrants now attempted to cross. They found, according to the native annalist, a rude bridge in a huge grape-vine which trailed its length across the stream. Over this a part of the company passed, and then, unfortunately, the vine broke. The residue, unable to cross, remained on the hither side, and became afterwards the enemies of those who had passed over. Cusick anticipates that his story of the grape-vine may seem to some incredible; but he asks, with amusing simplicity, "why more so than that the Israelites should cross the Red Sea on dry land?" That the precise incident, thus frankly admitted to be of a miraculous character, really took place, we are not required to believe. But that emigrants of the Huron-Iroquois stock penetrated southward along the Allegheny range, and that some of them remained near the river of that name, is undoubted fact. Those who thus remained were known by various names, mostly derived from one root--Andastes, Andastogues, Conestogas, and the like-- and bore a somewhat memorable part in Iroquois and Pennsylvanian history. Those who continued their course beyond the river found no place sufficiently inviting to arrest their march until they arrived at the fertile vales which spread, intersected by many lucid streams, between the Roanoke and the Neuse rivers. Here they fixed their abode, and became the ancestors of the powerful Tuscarora nation. In the early part of the eighteenth century, just before its disastrous war with the colonies, this nation, according to the Carolina surveyor, Lawson, numbered fifteen towns, and could set in the field a force of twelve hundred warriors.

The Eries, who dwelt west of the Senecas, along the southern shore of the lake which now retains their name, were, according to Cusick, an offshoot of the Seneca tribe; and there is no reason for doubting the correctness of his statement. After their overthrow by the Iroquois, in 1656, many of the Eries were incorporated with the ancestral nation, and contributed, with other accessions from the Hurons and the Attiwandaronks, to swell its numbers far beyond those of the other nations of the confederacy.

To conclude this review of the Huron-Iroquois group, something further should be said about the fortunes of the parent tribe, or rather congeries of tribes,---for the Huron household, like the Iroquois, had become divided into several septs. Like the Iroquois, also, they have not lacked an annalist of their own race. A Wyandot Indian, Peter Doyentate Clarke, who emigrated with the main body of his people to the Indian Territory, and afterwards returned for a time to the remnant of his tribe dwelling near Amherstburg, in Canada, published in 1870 a small volume entitled "Origin and Traditional History of the Wyandots."[1] The English education of the writer, like that of the Tuscarora historian, was defective; and it is evident that his people, in their many wanderings, had lost much of their legendary lore. But the fact that they resided in ancient times near the present site of Montreal, in close vicinity to the Iroquois (whom he styles, after their largest tribe, the Senecas), is recorded as a well-remembered portion of their history. The flight of the Wyandots to the northwest is declared to have been caused by a war which broke out between them and the Iroquois. This statement is opposed to the common opinion, which ascribes the expulsion of the Hurons from their eastern abode to the hostility of the Algonkins. It is, however, probably correct; for the Hurons retreated into the midst of the Algonkin tribes, with whom they were found by Champlain to be on terms of amity and even of alliance, while they were engaged in a deadly war with the Iroquois. The place to which they withdrew was a nook in the Georgian Bay, where their strongly palisaded towns and well-cultivated fields excited the admiration of the great French explorer. Their object evidently was to place as. wide a space as possible between themselves and their inveterate enemies. Unfortunately, as is well known, this precaution, and even the aid of their Algonkin and French allies, proved inadequate to save them. The story of their disastrous overthrow, traced by the masterly hand of Parkman, is one of the most dismal passages of aboriginal history.

The only people of this stock remaining to be noticed are the Attiwanda-ronks, or Neutral Nation. They dwelt south of the Hurons, on the northern borders of Lakes Erie and Ontario. They had, indeed, a few towns beyond those lakes, situated east of the Niagara river, between the Iroquois and the Eries. They received their name of Neutrals from the fact that in the war between the Iroquois and the Hurons they remained at peace with both parties. This policy, however, did not save them from the fate which

---

[1] Printed by Hunter, Rose & Co., of Toronto.

overtook their Huron friends. In the year 1650 the Iroquois set upon them, destroyed their towns, and dispersed the inhabitants, carrying off great numbers of them, as was their custom, to be incorporated with their own population. Of their language we only know that it differed but slightly from the Huron. [1] Whether they were an offshoot from the Hurons or from the Iroquois is uncertain. It is not unlikely that their separation from the parent stock took place earlier than that of the Iroquois, and that they were thus enabled for a time to avoid becoming embroiled in the quarrel between the two great divisions of their race.

---

[1] "Our Hurons call the Neutral Nation Attiwandaronk, meaning thereby 'People of a speech a little different.'"--Relation of 1641, p. 72. Bruyas, in his "Iroquois Root-words," gives us gawenda (or gawenna), speech, and gaRONKwestare, confusion of voices.

THE LEAGUE AND ITS FOUNDERS

How long the five kindred but independent tribes who were afterwards to compose the Iroquois confederacy remained isolated and apart from one another, is uncertain. That this condition endured for several centuries is a fact which cannot be questioned. Tradition here is confirmed by the evidence of language. We have good dictionaries of two of their dialects, the Canienga (or Mohawk) and the Onondaga, compiled two centuries ago by the Jesuit missionaries; and by comparing them with vocabularies of the same dialects, as spoken at the present day, we can ascertain the rate of change which prevails in their languages. judging by this test, the difference which existed between these two dialects in 1680 (when the Jesuit dictionaries were written) could hardly have arisen in less than four hundred years; and that which exists between them and the Tuscarora would demand a still longer time. Their traditions all affirm--what we should be prepared to believe--that this period was one of perpetual troubles. The tribes were constantly at war, either among themselves, or with the neighboring nations of their own and other stocks, Hurons, Andastes, Algonkins, Tuteloes, and even with the distant Cherokees.

There are reasons for believing that attempts were made during this period to combine the tribes, or some of them, in a federal alliance. But if such connections were formed, they proved only temporary leagues, which were dissolved when the dangers that had called them into being had passed away. A leader of peculiar qualities, aided by favoring circumstances, was able at last to bring about a more permanent union. There is no exact chronology by which the date of this important event can be ascertained; but the weight of evidence fixes it at about the middle of the fifteenth century. [1]

---

[1] The evidence on this point is given in the Appendix, note C. It should be mentioned that some portion of the following narrative formed part of a paper entitled "A Lawgiver of the Stone Age," which was read at the Cincinnati meeting of the American Association for the Advancement of Science, in August, 1882, and was published in the Proceedings of the meeting. The particulars comprised in it were drawn chiefly from notes gathered during many visits to the Reserve of the

At this time two great dangers, the one from without, the other from within, pressed upon these tribes. The Mohegans, or Mohicans, a powerful Algonkin people, whose settlements stretched along the Hudson river, south of the Mohawk, and extended thence eastward into New England, waged a desperate war against them. In this war the most easterly of the Iroquois, the Caniengas and Oneidas, bore the brunt and were the greatest sufferers. On the other hand, the two western nations, the Senecas and Cayugas, had a peril of their own to encounter. The central nation, the Onondagas, were then under the control of a dreaded chief, whose name is variously given, Atotarho (or, with a prefixed particle, Thatotarho), Watatotahro, Tadodaho, according to the dialect of the speaker and the orthography of the writer. He was a man of great force of character and of formidable qualities--haughty, ambitious, crafty and bold--a determined and successful warrior, and at home, so far as the constitution of an Indian tribe would allow a stern and remorseless tyrant. He tolerated no equal. The chiefs who ventured to oppose him were taken off one after another by secret means, or were compelled to flee for safety to other tribes. His subtlety and artifices had acquired for him the reputation of a wizard. He knew, they say, what was going on at a distance as well as if he were present; and he could destroy his enemies by some magical art, while he himself was far away. In spite of the fear which he inspired, his domination would probably not have been endured by an Indian community, but for his success in war. He had made himself and his people a terror to the

---

Six Nations, on the Grand River, in Ontario, supplemented by information obtained in two visits to the Onondaga Reservation, in the State of New York, near Syracuse. My informants were the most experienced councillors, and especially the "wampum-keepers," the official annalists of their people. Their names, and some account of them, will be given in a subsequent chapter. It should be mentioned that while the histories received at the two localities were generally in close accord, thus furnishing a strong proof of the correctness with which they have been handed down, there were circumstances remembered at each place which had not been preserved at the other. The Onondagas, as was natural, retained a fuller recollection of the events which took place before the flight of Hiawatha to the Caniengas; while the annalists of the latter tribe were better versed in the subsequent occurrences attending the formation of the League. These facts should be borne in mind by any inquirer who may undertake to repeat or continue these investigations. When the narratives varied, as they sometimes did in minor particulars, I have followed that which seemed most in accordancc with the general tenor of the history and with the evidence furnished by the Book of Rites.

Cayugas and the Senecas. According to one account, he had subdued both of those tribes; but the record-keepers of the present-day do not confirm this statement, which indeed is not consistent with the subsequent history of the confederation.

The name Atotarho signifies "entangled." The usual process by which mythology, after a few generations, makes fables out of names, has not been wanting here. In the legends which the Indian story-tellers recount in winter, about their cabin fires, Atotarho figures as a being of preterhuman nature, whose head, in lieu of hair, is adorned with living snakes. A rude pictorial representation shows him seated and giving audience, in horrible state, with the upper part of his person enveloped by these writhing and entangled reptiles. [1]

But the grave Councillors of the Canadian Reservation, who recite his history as they have heard it from their fathers at every installation of a high chief, do not repeat these inventions of marvel-loving gossips, and only smile with good-humored derision when they are referred to.

There was at this time among the Onondagas a chief of high rank, whose name, variously written--Hiawatha, Hayenwatha, Ayonhwahtha, Taoung-watha--is rendered, "he who seeks the wampum belt." He had made himself greatly esteemed by his wisdom and his benevolence. He was now past middle age. Though many of his friends and relatives had perished by the machinations of Atotarho, he himself had been spared. The qualities which gained him general respect had, perhaps, not been without influence even on that redoubtable chief. Hiawatha had long beheld with grief the evils which afflicted not only his own nation, but all the other tribes about them, through the continual wars in which they were engaged, and the misgovernment and miseries at home which these wars produced. With much meditation he had elaborated in his mind the scheme of a vast confederation which would ensure universal peace. In the mere plan of a

---

[1] This picture and some other equally grotesque illustrations, produced in a primitive style of wood engraving, are prefixed to David Cusick's History of the Six Nations. The artist to whom we owe them was probably the historian himself. My accomplished friend, Mrs. E. A. Smith, whose studies have thrown much light upon the mythology and language p. 21 of the Iroquois nations, and especially of the Tuscaroras, was fortunate enough to obtain either the originals or early copies of these extraordinary efforts of native art.

confederation there was nothing new. There are probably few, if any, Indian tribes which have not, at one time or another, been members of a league or confederacy. It may almost be said to be their normal condition. But the plan which Hiawatha had evolved differed from all others in two particulars. The system which he devised was to be not a loose and transitory league, but a permanent government. While each nation was to retain its own council and its management of local affairs, the general control was to be lodged in a federal senate, composed of representatives elected by each nation, holding office during good behavior, and acknowledged as ruling chiefs throughout the whole confederacy. Still further, and more remarkably, the confederation was not to be a limited one. It was to be indefinitely expansible. The avowed design of its proposer was to abolish war altogether. He wished the federation to extend until all the tribes of men should be included in it, and peace should everywhere reign. Such is the positive testimony of the Iroquois themselves; and their statement, as will be seen, is supported by historical evidence.

Hiawatha's first endeavor was to enlist his own nation in the cause. He summoned a meeting of the chiefs and people of the Onondaga towns. The summons, proceeding from a chief of his rank and reputation, attracted a large concourse. "They came together," said the narrator, "along the creeks, from all parts, to the general council-fire." [1] But what effect the grand projects of the chief, enforced by the eloquence for which he was noted, might have had upon his auditors, could not be known. For there appeared among them a well-known figure, grim, silent and forbidding, whose terrible aspect overawed the assemblage. The unspoken displeasure of Atotarho was sufficient to stifle all debate, and the meeting dispersed. This result, which seems a singular conclusion of an Indian council--the most independent and free-spoken of all gatherings--is sufficiently explained by the fact that Atotarho had organized, among the more reckless warriors of his tribe, a band of unscrupulous partisans, who did his bidding without question, and took off by secret murder all persons against whom he bore a grudge. The knowledge that his followers were scattered

---

[1] The narrator here referred to was the Onondaga chief, Philip Jones, known in the council as Hanesehen (in Canienga, Enneserarenh), who, in October, 1875, with two other chiefs of high rank, and the interpreter, Daniel La Fort, spent an evening in explaining to me the wampum records preserved at "Onondaga Castle," and repeating the history of the formation of the confederacy. The later portions of the narrative were obtained principally from the chiefs of the Canadian Iroquois, as will be hereafter explained.

through the assembly, prepared to mark for destruction those who should offend him, might make the boldest orator chary of speech. Hiawatha alone was undaunted. He summoned a second meeting, which was attended by a smaller number, and broke up as before, in confusion, on Atotarho's appearance. The unwearied reformer sent forth his runners a third time; but the people were disheartened. When the day of the council arrived, no one attended. Then, continued the narrator, Hiawatha seated himself on the ground in sorrow. He enveloped his head in his mantle of skins, and remained for a long time bowed down in grief and thought. At length he arose and left the town, taking his course toward the southeast. He had formed a bold design. As the councils of his own nation were closed to him, he would have recourse to those of other tribes. At a short distance from the town (so minutely are the circumstances recounted) he passed his great antagonist, seated near a well-known spring, stern and silent as usual. No word passed between the determined representatives of war and peace; but it was doubtless not without a sensation of triumphant pleasure that the ferocious war-chief saw his only rival and opponent in council going into what seemed to be voluntary exile. Hiawatha plunged into the forest; he climbed mountains; he crossed a lake; he floated down the Mohawk river in a canoe. Many incidents of his journey are told, and in this part of the narrative alone some occurrences of a marvelous cast are related, even by the official historians. Indeed, the flight of Hiawatha from Onondaga to the country of the Caniengas is to the Five Nations what the flight of Mohammed from Mecca to Medina is to the votaries of Islam. It is the turning point of their history. In embellishing the narrative at this point, their imagination has been allowed a free course. Leaving aside these marvels, however, we need only refer here to a single incident, which may well enough have been of actual occurrence. A lake which Hiawatha crossed had shores abounding in small white shells. These he gathered and strung upon strings, which he disposed upon his breast, as a token to all whom he should meet that he came as a messenger of peace. And this, according to one authority, was the origin of wampum, of which Hiawatha was the inventor. That honor, however, is one which must be denied to him. The evidence of sepulchral relics shows that wampum was known to the mysterious Mound-builders, as well as in all succeeding ages. Moreover, if the significance of white wampum-strings as a token of peace had not been well known in his day, Hiawatha would not have relied upon them as a means of proclaiming his pacific purpose.

Early one morning he arrived at a Canienga town, the residence of the noted chief Dekanawidah, whose name, in point of celebrity, ranks in Iroquois tradition with those of Hiawatha and Atotarho. It is probable that he was known by reputation to Hiawatha, and not unlikely that they were related. According to one account Dekanawidah was an Onondaga, adopted among the Caniengas. Another narrative makes him a Canienga by birth. The probability seems to be that he was the son of an Onondaga father, who had been adopted by the Caniengas, and of a Canienga mother. That he was not of pure Canienga blood is shown by the fact, which is remembered, that his father had had successively three wives, one belonging to each of the three clans, Bear, Wolf, and Tortoise, which composed the Canienga nation. If the father had been of that nation (Canienga), he would have belonged to one of the Canienga clans, and could not then (according to the Indian law) have married into it. He bad seven sons, including Dekanawidah, who, with their families, dwelt together in one of the "long houses" common in that day among the Iroquois. These ties of kindred, together with this fraternal strength, and his reputation as a sagacious councillor, gave Dekanawidah great influence among his people. But, in the Indian sense, he was not the leading chief. This position belonged to Tekarihoken (better known in books as Tecariho-ga), whose primacy as the first chief of the eldest among the Iroquois nations was then, and is still, universally admitted. Each nation has always had a head-chief, to whom belonged the hereditary right and duty of lighting the council fire and taking the first place in public meetings. But among the Indians, as in other communities, hereditary rank and personal influence do not always, or indeed, ordinarily, go together. If Hiawatha could gain over Dekanawidah to his views, he would have done much toward the accomplishment of his purposes.

In the early dawn he seated himself on a fallen trunk, near the spring from which the inhabitants of the long house drew their water. Presently the wife of one of the brothers came out with a vessel of elm-bark, and approached the spring. Hiawatha sat silent and motionless. Something in his aspect awed the woman, who feared to address him. She returned to the house, and said to Dekanawidah, "A man, or a figure like a man, is seated by the spring, having his breast covered with strings of white shells." "It is a guest," said the chief to one of his brothers; "go and bring him in. We will. make him welcome." Thus Hiawatha and Dekanawidah. first met. They found in each other kindred spirits. The sagacity of the Canienga chief grasped at once the advantages of the proposed plan, and the two worked together in perfecting it, and in commending it to the people. After much discussion in council, the adhesion of the Canienga nation was secured. Dekanawidah then despatched two of his. brothers as ambassadors to the nearest tribe, the Oneidas, to lay the project before them. The Oneida nation is deemed to be a comparatively recent offshoot from the Caniengas. The difference of language is slight, showing that their separation was much later than that of the Onondagas. In the figurative speech of the Iroquois, the Oneida is the son, and the Onondaga is the brother, of the Canienga. Dekanawidah had good reason to expect that it would not prove difficult to win the consent of the Oneidas to the proposed scheme. But delay and deliberation mark all public acts of the Indians. The ambassadors found the leading chief, Odatsehte, at his town on the Oneida creek. He received their message in a friendly way, but required time for his people to consider it in council. "Come back in another day," he said to the messengers. In the political speech of the Indians, a day is understood to mean a year. The envoys carried back the reply to Dekanawidah and Hiawatha, who knew that they could do nothing but wait the prescribed time. After the lapse of a year, they repaired to the place of meeting. The treaty which initiated the great league was then and there ratified by the representatives of the Canienga and Oneida nations. The name of Odatsehte means "the quiver-bearer;" and as Atotarho, "the entangled," is fabled to have had his head wreathed with snaky locks, and as Hiawatha, "the wampum-seeker," is represented to have wrought shells into wampum, so the Oneida chief is reputed to have appeared at this treaty bearing at his shoulder a quiver full of arrows.

The Onondagas lay next to the Oneidas. To them, or rather to their terrible chief, the next application was made. The first meeting of Atotarho and Dekanawidah is a notable event in Iroquois history. At a later day, a native artist sought to represent it in an historical picture, which has been already referred to. Atotarho is seated in solitary and surly dignity, smoking a long pipe, his head and body encircled with contorted and angry serpents. Standing before him are two figures which cannot be mistaken. The foremost, a plumed and cinctured warrior, depicted as addressing the Onondaga chief, holds in his right hand, as a staff, his flint-headed spear, the ensign, it may be supposed, which marks him as the representative of the Caniengas, or "People of the Flint." Behind him another plumed figure bears in his hand a bow with arrows, and at his shoulder a quiver. Divested of its mythological embellishments, the picture rudely represents the interview which actually took place. The immediate result was unpromising. The Onondaga chief coldly refused to entertain the project, which he had already rejected when proposed by Hiawatha. The ambassadors were not discouraged. Beyond the Onondagas were scattered the villages of the Cayugas, a people described by the Jesuit missionaries, at a later day, as the most mild and tractable of the Iroquois. They were considered an offshoot of the Onondagas, to whom they bore the same filial relation which the Oneidas bore to the Caniengas. The journey of the advocates of peace through the forest to the Cayuga capital, and their reception, are minutely detailed in the traditionary narrative. The Cayugas, who had suffered from the prowess and cruelty of the Onondaga chief, needed little persuasion. They readily consented to come into the league, and their chief, Akahenyonk ("The Wary Spy"), joined the Canienga and Oneida representatives in a new embassy to the Onondagas. Acting probably upon the advice of Hiawatha, who knew better than any other the character of the community and the chief with whom they had to deal, they made proposals highly flattering to the self-esteem which was the most notable trait of both ruler and people. The Onondagas should be the leading nation of the confederacy. Their chief town should be the federal capital, where the great councils of the league should be held, and where its records should be preserved. The nation should be represented in the council by fourteen senators, while no other nation should have more than ten. And as the Onondagas should be the leading tribe, so Atotarho should be the leading chief. He alone should have the right of summoning the federal council, and no act of the council to which he objected should be valid. In other words, an absolute veto was given to him. To enhance his personal dignity, two high chiefs were appointed as his special aids and counsellors, his "Secretaries of State," so to speak. Other insignia of preëminence were to be possessed by him; and, in view of all these distinctions, it is not surprising that his successor, who two centuries later retained the same prerogatives, should have been occasionally styled by the English colonists "the Emperor of the Five Nations." It might seem, indeed, at first thought, that the founders of the confederacy had voluntarily placed themselves and their tribes in a position of almost abject subserviency to Atotarho and his followers. But they knew too well the qualities of their people to fear for them any political subjection. It was certain that when once the league was established, and its representatives had met in council, character and intelligence would assume their natural sway, and mere artificial rank and dignity would be little regarded. Atotarho and his people, however, yielded either to these specious offers, or to the pressure which the combined urgency of the three allied nations now brought to bear upon them. They finally accepted the league; and the great chief, who had originally opposed it, now naturally became eager to see it as widely extended as possible. He advised its representatives to go on at once to the westward, and enlist the populous Seneca towns, pointing out how this might best be done. This advice was followed, and the adhesion of the Senecas was secured by giving to their two leading chiefs, Kanyadariyo ("Beautiful Lake") and Shadekaronyes ("The Equal Skies"), the offices of military commanders of the confederacy, with the title of doorkeepers of the "Long-house," that being the figure by which the league was known.

The six national leaders who have been mentioned--Dekanawidah for the Caniengas, Odatsehte for the Oneidas, Atotarho for the Onondagas, Akahenyonk for the Cayugas, Kanyadariyo and Shadekaronyes for the two great divisions of the Senecas--met in convention near the Onondaga Lake, with Hiawatha for their adviser, and a vast concourse of their followers, to settle the terms and rules of their confederacy, and to nominate its first council. Of this council, nine members (or ten, if Dekanawidah be included) were assigned to the Caniengas, a like number to the Oneidas, fourteen to the lordly Onondagas, ten to the Cayugas, and eight to the Senecas. Except in the way of compliment, the number assigned to each nation was really of little consequence, inasmuch as, by the rule of the league, unanimity was exacted in all their decisions. This unanimity, however, did not require the suffrage of every member of the council. The representatives of each nation first deliberated apart upon the question proposed. In this separate council the majority decided; and the leading chief then expressed in the great council the voice of his nation. Thus the veto of Atotarho ceased at once to be peculiar to him, and became a right exercised by each of the allied nations. This requirement of unanimity, embarrassing as it might seem, did not prove to be so in practice. Whenever a question arose on which opinions were divided, its decision was either postponed, or some compromise was reached which left all parties contented.

The first members of the council were appointed by the convention--under what precise rule is unknown; but their successors came in by a method in which the hereditary and the elective systems were singularly combined, and in which female suffrage had an important place. When a chief died or (as sometimes happened) was deposed for incapacity or misconduct, some member of the same family succeeded him. Rank followed the female line; and this successor might be any descendant of the late chief's mother or grandmother--his brother, his cousin or his nephew--but never his son.

Among many persons who might thus be eligible, the selection was made in the first instance by a family council. In this council the "chief matron" of the family, a noble dame whose position and right were well defined, had the deciding voice. This remarkable fact is affirmed by the Jesuit missionary Lafitau, and the usage remains in full vigor among the Canadian Iroquois to this day.[1] If there are two or more members of the family who seem to have equal claims, the nominating matron sometimes declines to decide between them, and names them both or all, leaving the ultimate choice to the nation or the federal council. The council of the nation next considers the nomination, and, if dissatisfied, refers it back to the family for a new designation. If content, the national council reports the name of the candidate to the federal senate, in which resides the power of ratifying or rejecting the choice of the nation; but the power of rejection is rarely exercised, though that of expulsion for good cause is not unfrequently exerted. The new chief inherits the name of his predecessor. In this respect, as in some others, the resemblance of the Great Council to the English House of Peers is striking. As Norfolk succeeds to Norfolk, so Tekarihoken succeeds Tekarihoken. The great names of Hiawatha and Atotarho are still borne by plain farmer-councillors on the Canadian Reservation.

When the League was established, Hiawatha had been adopted by the Canienga nation as one of their chiefs. The honor in which he was held by them is shown by his position on the roll of councillors, as it has been handed down from the earliest times. As the Canienga nation is the "elder brother," the names of its chiefs are first recited. At the head of the list is the leading Canienga chief, Tekarihoken, who represents the noblest lineage of the Iroquois stock.

Next to him, and second on the roll, is the name of Hiawatha. That of his great colleague, Dekanawidah, nowhere appears. He was a member of the

---

[1] La dignité de chef est perpétuelle et héréditaire dans sa Cabane, passant toujours aux enfans de ses tantes, de ses sœurs, ou de ses nièces du côté maternel. Dès que l'arbre est tombé, il fault, disent ils, le relever. La matrone, qui a la principale autorité, après en avoir conferé avec ceux de sa Cabane, en confère de nouveau avec ceux de sa Tribu [clan], à qui elle fait agréer celui qu'elle a choisi pour succéder, ce qui lui est assez libre. Elle n'a pas toujours égard au droit d'ainesse, et d'ordinaire, elle prend celui qui paroit le plus propre A soûtenir ce rang par ses bonnes qualités."--Lafitau: Mœurs des Sauvages Ameriquains, p. 471.

first council but he forbade his people to appoint a successor to him. Let the others. have successors," he said proudly, "for others can advise you like them. But I aim the founder of your league, and no one else can do what I have done." [1]

The boast was not unwarranted. Though planned by another, the structure had been reared mainly by his labors. But the Five Nations, while yielding abundant honor to the memory of Dekanawidah, have never regarded him with the same affectionate reverence which has always clung to the name of Hiawatha. His tender and lofty wisdom, his wide-reaching benevolence, and his fervent appeals to their better sentiments, enforced by the eloquence of which he was master, touched chords in the popular heart which have continued to respond until this day. Fragments of the speeches in which he addressed the council and the people of the league are still remembered and repeated. The fact that the league only carried out a part of the grand design which he had in view is constantly affirmed. Yet the failure was not due to lack of effort. In pursuance of his original purpose, when the league was firmly established, envoys were sent to other tribes to urge them to join it, or at least to become allies. One of these embassies penetrated to the distant Cherokees, the hereditary enemies of the Iroquois nations. For some reason with which we are not acquainted, perhaps the natural suspicion or vindictive pride of that powerful commu-

---

[1] In Mr. Morgan's admirable work, "The League of the Iroquois," the list of Councillors (whom he styles sachems), comprises the name of Dekanawidah--in his orthography, Dagänowedä. During my last visit to my lamented friend (in September, 1880), when we examined together my copy of the then newly discovered Book of Rites, in which he was greatly interested, this point was considered. The original notes which he made for his work were examined. It appeared that in the list as it was first written by him, from the dictation of a well-informed Seneca chief, the name of Dekanawidah was not comprised. A later, but erroneous suggestion, from another source, led him to believe that his first informant was mistaken, or that he had misunderstood him, and to substitute the name of Dekanawidah for the somewhat similar name of Shatekariwate (in Seneca. Sadekeiwadeh), which stands third on the roll, immediately following that of Hiawatha. The term sachem, it may be added, is an Algonkin word, and one which Iroquois speakers have a difficulty in pronouncing. Their own name for a member of their Senate is Royaner, derived from the root yaner, noble, and precisely equivalent in meaning to the English "nobleman" or "lord," as applied to a member of the House of Peers. It is the word by which the missionaries have rendered the title "Lord" in the New Testament.

nity, this mission was a failure. Another, despatched to the western Algonkins, had better success. A strict alliance was formed with the far-spread Ojibway tribes, and was maintained inviolate for at least two hundred years, until at length the influence of the French, with the sympathy of the Ojibways for the conquered Hurons, undid to some extent, though not entirely, this portion of Hiawatha's work.

His conceptions were beyond his time, and beyond ours; but their effect, within a limited sphere, was very great. For more than three centuries the bond which he devised held together the Iroquois nations in perfect amity. It proved, moreover, as he intended, elastic. The territory of the Iroquois, constantly extending as their united strength made itself felt, became the "Great Asylum" of the Indian tribes. Of the conquered Eries and Hurons, many hundreds were received and adopted among their conquerors. The Tuscaroras, expelled by the English from North Carolina, took refuge with the Iroquois, and became the sixth nation of the League. From still further south, the Tuteloes and Saponies, of Dakota stock, after many wars with the Iroquois, fled to them from their other enemies, and found a cordial welcome. A chief still sits in the council as a representative of the Tuteloes, though the tribe itself has been swept away by disease, or absorbed in the larger nations.

Many fragments of tribes of Algonkin lineage--Delawares, Nanticokes, Mohegans, Mississagas--sought the same hospitable protection, which never failed them. Their descendants still reside on the Canadian Reservation, which may well be styled an aboriginal "refuge of nations," affording a striking evidence in our own day of the persistent force of a great idea, when embodied in practical shape by the energy of a master mind.

The name by which their constitution or organic law s known among them is kayánerenh, to which the epitaph kowa, "great," is frequently added. This word, kayánerenh, is sometimes rendered "law," or "league," but its proper meaning seems to be "peace." It is used in this sense by the missionaries, in their translations of the scriptures and the prayer-book. In such expressions as the "Prince of Peace," "the author of peace," "give peace in our time," we find kayánerenh employed with this meaning. Its root is yaner, signifying "noble," or "excellent," which yields, among many derivatives, kayánere, "goodness," and kayánerenh, "peace," or "peacefulness." The national hymn of the confederacy, sung whenever their "Condoling Council" meets, commences with a verse referring to their league, which is literally rendered, "We come to greet and thank the PEACE" (kayánerenh). When the list of their ancient chiefs, the fifty original councillors, is chanted in the closing litany of the meeting, there is heard from time to time, as the leaders of each clan are named, an outburst of praise, in the words--

This was the roll of you--
You that combined in the work,
You that completed the work,
The GREAT PEACE." (Kayánerenh-kowa.)

The regard of Englishmen for their Magna Charta and Bill of Rights, and that of Americans for their national Constitution, seem weak in comparison with the intense gratitude and reverence of the Five Nations for the "Great Peace," which Hiawatha and his colleagues established for them.

Of the subsequent life of Hiawatha, and of his death, we have no sure information. The records of the Iroquois are historical, and not biographical. As Hiawatha had been made a chief among the Caniengas, he doubtless continued to reside with that nation. A tradition, which is in itself highly probable, represents him as devoting himself to the congenial work of clearing away the obstructions in the streams which intersect the country then inhabited by the confederated nations, and which formed the chief means of communication between them. That he thus, in some measure, anticipated the plans of De Witt Clinton and his associates, on a smaller scale, but perhaps with a larger statesmanship, we may be willing enough to believe. A wild legend recorded by some writers, but not told of him by the Canadian Iroquois, and apparently belonging to their ancient mythology, gives him an apotheosis, and makes him ascend to heaven in a white canoe. It may be proper to dwell for a moment on the singular complication of mistakes which has converted this Indian reformer and statesman into a mythological personage.

When by the events of the Revolutionary war the original confederacy was broken up, the larger portion of the people followed Brant to Canada. The refugees comprised nearly the whole of the Caniengas, and the greater part of the Onondagas and Cayugas, with many members of the other nations. In Canada their first proceeding was to reëstablish, as far as possible, their ancient league, with all its laws and ceremonies. The Onondagas had brought with them most of their wampum records, and the

Caniengas jealously preserved the memories of the federation, in whose formation they had borne a leading part. The history of the league continued to be the topic of their orators whenever a new chief was installed into office. Thus the remembrance of the facts has been preserved among them with much clearness and precision, and with little admixture of mythological elements. With the fragments of the tribes which remained on the southern side of the Great Lakes the case was very different. A feeble pretence was made, for a time, of keeping up the semblance of the old confederacy; but except among the Senecas, who, of all the Five Nations, had had least to do with the formation of the league, the ancient families which had furnished the members of their senate, and were the conservators of their history, had mostly fled to Canada or the West. The result was that among the interminable stories with which the common people beguile their winter nights, the traditions of Atotarho and Hiawatha became intermingled with the legends of their mythology. An accidental similarity, in the Onondaga dialect, between the name of Hiawatha and that of one of their ancient divinities, led to a confusion between the two, which has misled some investigators. This deity bears, in the sonorous Canienga tongue, the name of Taronhiawagon, meaning "the Holder of the Heavens." The Jesuit missionaries style him "the great god of the Iroquois." Among the Onondagas of the present day, the name is abridged to Taonhiawagi, or Tahiawagi. The confusion between this name and that of Hiawatha (which, in another form, is pronounced Tahionwatha) seems to have begun more than a century ago; for Pyrlæus, the Moravian missionary, heard among the Iroquois (according to Heckewelder) that the person who first proposed the league was an ancient Mohawk, named Thannawege. Mr. J. V. H. Clarke, in his interesting History of Onondaga, makes the name to have been originally Ta-oun-ya-wat-ha, and describes the bearer as "the deity who presides over fisheries and hunting-grounds." He came down from heaven in a white canoe, and after sundry adventures, which remind one of the labors of Hercules, assumed the name of Hiawatha (signifying, we are told, "a very wise man "), and dwelt for a time as an ordinary mortal among men, occupied in works of benevolence. Finally, after founding the confederacy and bestowing many prudent counsels upon the people, he returned to the skies by the same conveyance in which he had descended. This legend, or, rather, congeries of intermingled legends, was communicated by Clark to Schoolcraft, when the latter was compiling his "Notes on the Iroquois." Mr. Schoolcraft, pleased with the poetical cast of the story, and the euphonious name, made confusion worse confounded by transferring the hero to a distant region and identifying him with Manabozho, a fantastic divinity of the Ojibways. Schoolcraft's volume, which he chose to entitle "The Hiawatha Legends," has not in it a single fact or fiction relating either to Hiawatha himself or to the Iroquois deity Taronhiawagon. Wild Ojibway stories concerning Manabozho and his comrades form the staple of its contents. But it is to this collection that we owe the charming poem of Longfellow; and thus, by an extraordinary fortune, a grave Iroquois lawgiver of the fifteenth century has become, in modern literature, an Ojibway demigod, son of the West Wind, and companion of the tricksy Paupukkeewis, the boastful Iagoo, and the strong Kwasind. If a Chinese traveler, during the middle ages, inquiring into the history and religion of the western nations, had confounded King Alfred with King Arthur, and both with Odin, he would not have, made a more preposterous confusion of names and characters than that which has hitherto disguised the genuine personality of the great Onondaga reformer. [1]

About the main events of his history, and about his character and purposes, there can be no reasonable doubt. We have the wampum belts which he handled, and whose simple hieroglyphics preserve the memory of the public acts in which he took part. We have, also, in the Iroquois "Book of Rites," which in the present volume is given in its original form, a still more clear and convincing testimony to the character both of the legislator and of the people for whom his institutions were designed. This book, sometimes called the "Book of the Condoling Council," might properly enough be styled an Iroquois Veda. It comprises the speeches, songs, and other ceremonies, which, from the earliest period of the confederacy, have composed the proceedings of their council when a deceased chief is lamented and his successor is installed in office. The fundamental laws of the league, a list of their ancient towns, and the names of the chiefs who constituted their first council, chanted in a kind of litany, are also comprised in the collection. The contents, after being preserved in memory, like the Vedas, for many generations, were written down by desire of the chiefs, when their language was first reduced to writing; and the book is therefore more than a century old. Its language, archaic when written, is now partly obsolete, and is fully understood by only a few of the oldest chiefs. It is a genuine Indian composition, and must be accepted as disclosing the true character of its authors. The result is remarkable enough. Instead of a race of rude and ferocious warriors, we find in this

---

[1] This subject is further discussed in the Appendix, Note D.

book a kindly and affectionate people, full of sympathy for their friends in distress, considerate to their women, tender to their children, anxious for peace, and imbued with a profound reverence for their constitution and its authors. We become conscious of the fact that the aspect in which these Indians have presented themselves to the outside world has been in a large measure deceptive and factitious. The ferocity, craft and cruelty, which have been deemed their leading traits, have been merely the natural accompaniments of wars of self-preservation, and no more indicated their genuine character than the war-paint, plume and tomahawk of the warrior displayed the customary guise in which he appeared among his own people. The cruelties of war, when war is a struggle for national existence, are common to all races. The persistent desire for peace, pursued for centuries in federal unions, and in alliances and treaties with other nations, has been manifested by few as steadily as by the countrymen of Hiawatha. The sentiment of universal brotherhood which directed their polity has never been so fully developed in any branch of the Aryan race, unless it may be found incorporated in the religious quietism of Buddha and his followers.

THE BOOK OF RITES

FOR a proper appreciation of this peculiar composition, some further particulars respecting its origin and character will be needed. During my earlier visits to the Reserve of the Six Nations, near Brantford, I had heard of an Indian book which was used at their "Condoling Councils," the most important of their many public gatherings. But it was not until the month of September, 1879, that I had an opportunity of seeing the work. At that time two copies of the book were brought to me by the official holders, two of the principal chiefs of the confederacy. One of these was Chief John "Smoke" Johnson, who for many years had held the high office of Speaker of the Great Council, though, of late, yielding to age and infirmity, he has withdrawn from the public performance of its duties. His second name is a rude rendering of his truly poetical Indian appellation, Sakayengwaraton, or "Disappearing Mist." It signifies properly, I was told, the haze which rises from the ground in an autumn morning and vanishes as the day advances. His English name, and, in part, his blood, Chief Johnson derives from no less distinguished an ancestor than Sir William Johnson, who played so notable a part in colonial history during the last century, and who exercised, perhaps, a greater influence on the destiny of the Iroquois than any other individual since the formation of their confederacy. To him, indeed, may be ascribed the distinction, such as it is, of destroying the work which Hiawatha and Dekanawidah had founded. But for the influence over the Indians which he had acquired, and was able to bequeath to others, it is probable that the Six Nations would have remained neutral during the Revolutionary War, and the disruption of their League would not have taken place. Yet there can be no doubt that he was sincerely attached to them, and desired their good. Unfortunately for them, they held, as was natural, only the second place in his affections. He was, by 4d option, an Iroquois chief, but his first allegiance was due to his native country, to whose interests, both in the war with France and in the separation which he foresaw between England and her colonies, he did not hesitate to sacrifice the welfare of his red brethren. Against his subtle arts and overmastering energy the wisest of their statesmen, worthy successors of the great founders of their constitution, strove in vain, on each occasion, to maintain that neutrality which was evidently the true policy of their people. [1]

Sakayengwaraton is not an elected chief, nor does he bear one of the hereditary titles of the Great Council, in which he holds so distinguished a station. Indeed, his office is one unknown to the ancient constitution of the Kanonsionni. It is the creation of the British Government, to which he owes, with the willing consent of his own people, his rank and position in the Council. The Provincial administrators saw the need of a native official who should be, like the Speaker of the English House of Commons, the mouthpiece of the Council, and the intermediary between it and the representative of the Crown. The grandson of Sir William Johnson was known as a brave warrior, a capable leader, and an eloquent speaker. In the war of 1812, at the early age of twenty, he bad succeeded an elder brother in the command of the Indian contingent, and had led his dusky followers with so much skill and intrepidity as to elicit high praise from the English commander. His eloquence was noted, even among a race of orators. I can well believe what I have heard of its effects, as even in his old age, when an occasion has for a moment aroused his spirit, I have not known whether most to admire the nobleness and force of his sentiments and reasoning, or the grace and flowing ease with which he delivered the stately periods of his sonorous language. He has been a worthy successor of the distinguished statesmen, Garagontieh, Garangula, Decanasora, Canasatego, Logan, and others, who in former years guided the destinies of his people. He is considered to have a better knowledge of the traditions and ancient usages of the Six Nations than any other member of the tribes, and is the only man now living who can tell the meaning of every word of the "Book of Rites."

The other chief to whom I have referred is the Onondaga Councillor who is known to the whites as John Buck, but who bears in council the name of Skanawati ("Beyond the River"), one of the fifty titular names which have descended from the time of Hiawatha. He is the official keeper of the "wampum records" of the confederacy, an important trust, which, to his knowledge, has been in his family for at least four generations. His rank, his character, and his eloquence make him now, virtually, the Iroquois premier--an office which, among the Six Nations, as among the Athenians

---

[1] For the confirmation of these statements see the excellent biographies of Sir William Johnson and Joseph Brant, by Wm. L. Stone, passim.

The Iroquois Book of Rites

of old and the English of modern days, is both unknown to the constitution and essential to its working. His knowledge of the legends and customs of his people is only inferior to that of the more aged Speaker of the Council.

The account which Chief J. S. Johnson gave me of the book may be briefly told. The English missionaries reduced the Canienga language to writing in the early part of the last century. The Jesuit fathers, indeed, had learned and written the language--which they styled the Iroquois--fifty years before; but it does not appear that they had instructed any of the Indians in the art of writing it, as their successors in the Eastern Province have since done. The English missionaries took pains to do this. The liturgy of their church was printed in the Mohawk tongue, at New York, as early as the year 1714. [1] By the middle of the century there were many members of the tribe who could write in the well-devised orthography of the missionaries-- an orthography which anticipated in most points the well known "Pickering alphabet," now generally employed in writing the Indian languages of North America. The chiefs of the Great Council, at once conservative and quick to learn, saw the advantages which would accrue from preserving, by this novel method, the forms of their most important public duty--that of creating new chiefs--and the traditions connected with their own body. They caused the ceremonies, speeches and songs, which together made up the proceedings of the Council when it met for the two purposes, always combined, of condolence and induction, to be written down in the words in which they had been preserved in memory for many generations. A Canienga chief, named David, a friend of Brant, is said to have accomplished the work. In Stone's Life of Sir William Johnson, mention is made of a Mohawk chief, "David of Schoharie," who, in May, 1757, led a troop of Indians from his town to join the forces under Sir William, in his expedition to Crown Point, to repel the French invaders. [2] Brant appears to have been in this expedition. [3] It is highly probable that in Chief David of Schoharie we have the compiler, or rather the scribe, of this "Iroquois Veda."

The copy of this book which Chief J. S. Johnson possessed was made by himself, under the following circumstances: During the prevalence of the

---

[1] This date is given in the preface to the Mohawk Prayer-book of 1787. This first version of the liturgy was printed under the direction of the Rev. Wm. Andrews, the missionary of the "New England Society."
[2] Life of Sir William Johnson, Vol. II, p. 29.
[3] Ibid., p. 174.

Asiatic cholera, in 1832, the tribes on the Reserve suffered severely. Chief Johnson, then a young man and not yet a leader in the Great Council, was active in attending on the sick. He was called to visit an aged chief, who was not expected to live. The old chief informed him that he had this book in his possession, and advised him, as he was one of the few who could write the language, to make a copy of it, lest by any accident the original should be lost. Johnson followed this advice, and copied the book on loose sheets of paper, from which he afterwards transcribed it into a small unbound book, resembling a schoolboy's copy-book. He states that the original book contained, besides the ceremonies of the Condoling Council, an addition by a later hand, comprising some account of the more recent history of the Six Nations, and particularly of their removal from New York to Canada. This portion of it he unfortunately omitted to copy, and shortly afterwards the book itself was destroyed, when the house of the old chief was accidentally burned.

The other copy which I transcribed was held by Chief John Buck, in his official capacity of record-keeper. It is written in a somewhat different orthography. The syllables are separated, as in the usual style of Indian hymnbooks, and some of the words, particularly the proper names, show by their forms that the person who copied the book was, an Onondaga. The copy was evidently not made from that of Chief Johnson, as it supplies some omissions in that copy. On the other hand, it omits some matters, and, in particular, nearly all the adjurations and descriptive epithets which form the closing litany accompanying the list of hereditary councillors. The copy appears, from a memorandum written in it, to have been made by one "John Green," who, it seems, was formerly a pupil of the Mohawk Institute at Brantford. It bears the date of November, 1874. I could not learn where he found his original.

The translation has been made from the dictation of Chief J. S. Johnson, who explained the meaning of the archaic words in the modern Canienga speech. This was interpreted in English by his son, Chief George H. M. Johnson, and afterwards more fully elucidated by my esteemed friend, the Rev. Isaac Bearfoot, who kindly came from his parish, at Point Edward (near Sarnia), to the Reserve, to assist me in this work. Mr. Bearfoot is an Onondaga by birth, but a Canienga by adoption, and has a thorough knowledge of the Canienga language. He prepared the revised edition of the hymnbook in that language, which is now used on the Reserve. He is a good English scholar, and, having been educated in Toronto for the ministry, has filled for some years, with much acceptance, the office of pastor to a white congregation of the Church of England. I am greatly indebted to him for his judicious assistance, and, finally, for a complete revision of the entire version of the Canienga portion of the book.

To my friend Chief George Johnson I am under still greater obligations. Mr. Johnson, as has been stated, is the son of Chief J. S. Johnson, and is himself a high chief of the Canienga nation. He bears in the Great Council the name of Teyonhehkwen (otherwise spelt Deyonheghgonh), meaning "Double Life," one of the titular names which were borne by the companions of Hiawatha and Atotarho in the first council. He succeeded in this title, according to the rules of the confederacy, his maternal uncle, on the nomination of his mother, as the chief matron of the family. Mr. Johnson is an educated gentleman. In early life he was a pupil of the English missionaries. He now holds the position of Government Interpreter for the Six Nations, and is, in fact, the chief executive officer of the Canadian government on the Reserve. His duties have several times brought him into collision with the white ruffians who formerly infested the Reserve, and from whom he has on two occasions suffered severe injuries, endangering his life. His courage and firmness, however, have been finally successful in subduing this mischief, and the Reserve is now as secure and as free from disorder as any part of Canada. To Chief George Johnson's assistance and encouragement I owe most of the information contained in these pages, and I am glad to have an opportunity of paying him this tribute of respect and gratitude.

The second or supplementary part of the Book, which is in the Onondaga dialect, was found on the small Reservation in the State of New York, near Syracuse, where a feeble remnant of the great Onondaga nation still cling to the home of their forefathers. In October, 1875, during my first visit to Onondaga Castle, as this Reservation is called, I obtained from the intelligent interpreter, Daniel La Fort-a son of the distinguished chief Abram La Fort (Dehatkatons), who is commemorated in Clark's "Onondaga"--a list of the original councillors in the Onondaga dialect, and also a copy, in the same dialect, of the "Condoling Song," which I had heard sung on the Canadian Reserve, and which I afterwards found in the Canienga Book of Rites. He read them to me from a small manuscript book, in which, as I then supposed, he had noted them for his own convenience. When I afterwards discovered the Canienga book, it occurred to me that I might have been mistaken on this point, and that the manuscript from which he read was possibly a copy of the Book of Rites in the Onondaga dialect. To clear up this point, I again visited Onondaga Castle, in September, 1880. I then found, to my great gratification, that his book was not a copy, but a valuable addition, or rather an essential complement, to the Canienga book. The last-named book comprises the speeches which are addressed by the representatives of the three elder nations to the younger members of the League, whenever a chief who belonged to the latter is lamented. The Onondaga book, on the other hand, gives us the exhortations which are addressed by the younger nations to the elder when a chief of the latter is mourned. The circumstance to which it owes its preservation on the Onondaga Reserve is easily explained. Of late years, since the chieftainships among the New York Senecas and Tuscaroras have been made purely elective offices, the only body of Indians in that State among whom the original system of mingled descent and appointment has been retained is the remnant of the intensely conservative Onondagas. Among these, in spite of missionary efforts continued for two centuries, paganism still lingers, and chiefs are still "raised up" as nearly as possible after the ancient fashion. When a chief dies, the members of his family or clan select another, who is presented to the national council for induction. The ceremonies of condolence, with which the proceedings commence, are modeled after the primitive form. As the Onondagas were one of the elder nations, the addresses of condolence must proceed from a younger brother. Fortunately for this purpose, a few Oneidas reside on the Reserve, among whom is a single chief, by name Abram Hill. To him is committed the duty of representing the "younger brothers" on this occasion, and with it the charge of the wampum strings, which are produced occasionally as the ceremony proceeds, each string representing one section or topic of the condoling address.

La Fort said that he had copied his book from a manuscript in his father's handwriting. This manuscript, unfortunately, was lost, and he could not say whether his father had first written it down from memory, or had merely transcribed it from an earlier composition. However this may have been, the substance of the composition undoubtedly dates from a period preceding the disruption of the confederacy. The language, indeed, so far as can be judged from the very irregular orthography, is modern. If, as there is reason to suppose, the composition is ancient, it has evidently undergone a "revision" at the hands of the later copyists. In former times, as we know from the Jesuit vocabularies, the sound of r existed in the Onondaga dialect. Since their day this sound has disappeared from it entirely. In La Fort's manuscript the letter frequently occurred, but always, as his pronunciation showed, either as a diacritical sign following the vowel a, to give to that vowel the sound of a in "far," or else as representing itself this vowel sound. Thus the syllable which should properly be written sa was written by La Fort either sar or sr. But, though the language is modern, the speeches themselves, as I am assured by Chief John Buck, are precisely those which are still in use among his people in Canada, and which are believed to have been preserved in memory from the days of their forefathers. [1]

The translation of La Fort's book was procured from him and another educated member of his tribe; but there was not time to obtain all the elucidations needed to ensure precise verbal accuracy throughout.

---

[1] The disappearance of a vocal element from a language is a phenomenon with which etymologists are familiar. The loss of the Greek digamma is a well-known instance. The harsh guttural, resembling the German ch, which formerly existed in the English language, has vanished from it, leaving its traces in the uncouth orthography of such words as plough, high, though, and the like. Within the past three centuries the sound of l has been lost from many words, such as walk, talk, balm and calm. The sound of r is disappearing from a large portion of the language. In ordinary speech, arm rhymes with calm, morning with fawning, higher with Sophia. Modern French, as is well known, has attained its present euphony through the disappearance of consonantal elements from many words in which they formerly existed.

THE CONDOLING COUNCIL.--CLANS AND CLASSES

THE name usually given to the Book of Rites, or rather to its contents, is, in the Canienga dialect, Okayondónghsera Yondénnase (or in the French missionary orthography, Okaiontonhsera Iontennase), which maybe rendered "Ancient Rites of the Condoling Council."[1] Among the many councils, civil and religious, tribal and federal, in which the public spirit and social temper of the Iroquois found their most congenial and most popular mode of display, the Yondennase, the Condoling (or Mourning) Council, held the highest rank. It was, in a certain way, typical of the whole, and comprised the elements of all the other councils. In its earlier form this council was not peculiar to the Iroquois. We know, from the Jesuit reports, that it was the custom of the Hurons to hold a public lamentation for the death of a chief, and at the same time to appoint another who should take his place and assume his name. But that which among the Hurons was merely a tribal custom became, in the Iroquois, form of government, an important institution, essential to the maintenance of their state. By the ordinances of their League, it was required that the number of their federal senate should be maintained undiminished. On the death of one of its members, it was the duty of the nation to which he belonged to notify the other nations of the event, and of the time and place at which he would be lamented and his successor installed. The notice was given in the usual manner, by official messengers, who bore for credentials certain strings of wampum, appropriate to the occasion. The place of meeting was commonly the chief town of the nation which had suffered the loss. In this nation a family council, under the presidency, and subject, indeed (as has been shown), to the controlling decision, of the chief matron of the deceased senator's kindred--usually his mother, if she survived him--was in the meantime convened to select his successor. The

---

[1] Okaiontonhsera is a substantive derived from ahaion, old, or ancient. The termination sera gives it an abstract sense. "The antiquities," or rather "the ancientnesses," is the nearest literal rendering which our language allows. Iontennase is a verbal form, derived from kitenre (in Bruyas, gentenron) to pity, or sympathize with. It may be rendered "they who sympathize," or "the condolers." Both words, however, have acquired a special meaning in their application to these ceremonies.

selection must be approved both by his clan and by his nation; but as their sentiments were generally known beforehand, this approval was rarely withheld. Indeed, the mischief resulting from an unsuitable choice was always likely to be slight; for both the national council and the federal senate had the right of deposing any member who was found unqualified for the office.

At the appointed day the chiefs of the other nations approached the place of meeting. A multitude of their people, men and women, usually accompanied them, prepared to take part both in the exhibitions of grief and in the festivities which always followed the installation of the new councillor. The approaching chiefs halted when they reached the border of the "opening," or cleared space surrounding the town. Here took place the "preliminary ceremony," styled in the Book of Rites, "Deyughnyonkwarakda," a word which means simply "at the edge of the woods." At this point a fire was kindled, a pipe was lighted and passed around with much formality, and an address of welcome was made by the principal chief of the inviting nation. The topics of this address comprised a singular mixture of congratulation and condolence, and seem to have been prescribed forms, which had come down from immemorial antiquity, as appropriate to the occasion.

The guests were then formally conducted--"led by the hand," as the Book recites--to the Council House of the town. They seem, anciently at least, to have advanced in the order of their clans. The towns belonging to the Wolf clan were first enumerated--probably as the chiefs belonging to them took their plates--then the towns of the Tortoise clan (or double clan, as it is styled), and finally those of the Bear clan. In all, twenty-three towns are named. Five of them are expressly stated to have been "added lately." The residue are supposed to be the names of the towns in which the people of the Five Nations resided at the time when the confederacy was formed, though this point is uncertain. That few of these can now be identified, is what would naturally be expected. It is well known that the Indians had the custom of removing their towns from time to time, at intervals varying from ten to twenty years, as the fuel in their neighborhood became exhausted, and as the diminished crops under their primitive mode of agriculture showed the need of fresher soil. Only those villages would be permanent whose localities offered some special advantages, as fortresses, fishing places, or harbors.[1]

This list of towns has another peculiarity which arrests the attention. It apparently comprises all the towns of the League, but these are divided among only three clans, those of the Wolf, the Tortoise and the Bear. The other clans of the confederacy are not once named in the book. Yet there are indications which show that when the list of chiefs which concludes the book was written, at a date long after this list of towns was first recited, other clans existed in three of the nations. This is an important point, which merits further consideration. Those who have read the admirable account of the "League of the Iroquois," by Morgan, and his philosophic work on "Ancient Society," are aware that he has brought out and elucidated with much clearness and force the nature and results of the remarkable clan system which prevails among the North American Indians. It is not universal, as it does not seem to be known among the widely scattered bands of the Crees and the Athapascans, or among the Indians of Oregon.[2] It was found, however, among the great majority of tribes in the region north of Mexico and east of the Rocky Mountains, and was sufficiently alike in all to indicate a common origin. Mr. Morgan finds this origin in a kinship, real or supposed, among the members of each clan. He considers the clan, or gens, and not the single family, to be the natural unit of primitive society. It is, in his view, a stage through which the human race passes in its progress from the savage state to civilization. It is difficult, however, to reconcile this theory with the fact that among some races, as for example, the Polynesian and Feejeean, which are in precisely the same stage of social advancement as the North American Indians, this institution is unknown; and even among the Indians, as has been said, it is not everywhere found. There are many indications which seem to show that the system is merely an artificial arrangement, instituted for social convenience. It is natural, in the sense that the desire for association is natural to man, The sentiment is one which manifests itself alike in all stages of society. The guilds of the middle ages, the masonic and other secret brotherhoods, religious organizations, trade unions, clubs, and even political parties, are all manifestations of this associative instinct. The Indian clan was simply a brotherhood, an aggregate of persons united by a common tie, sometimes of origin, sometimes merely of locality. These

---

[1] See Appendix, note E.
[2] See Ancient Society, pp. 167, 175, 177.

brotherhoods were not permanent, but were constantly undergoing changes, forming, dividing, coalescing, vanishing. The names of many of them show their recent origin. The Chicasas have a "Spanish clan." [1] The Shawnees had a "Horse clan." [2] The Iroquois, of Eastern Canada, made up of fragments of all the Five Nations, had an "Onondaga clan," and an "Oneida clan." [3] It is a curious fact that, as Mr. Morgan states, "the Iroquois claim to have originated a division of the people into tribes [clans or gentes] as a means of creating new relationships, to bind the people more firmly together. It is further asserted by them that they forced or introduced this social organization among the Cherokees, the Chippeways (Massasaugas) and several other Indian nations, with whom, in ancient times, they were in constant intercourse." "The fact," he adds, "that this division of the people of the same nation into tribes does not prevail generally among our Indian races, favors the assertions of the Iroquois." [4] Further inquiry and reflection led this distinguished investigator to take a totally different view, and to go to what may be deemed the opposite extreme of regarding this clan system as an essential stage in the growth of human society.

There can be no question that an idea of kinship pervaded the clan system, and was its ruling element. It may, in many instances, have been purely imaginary and, so to speak, figurative, like the "brotherhood" of our secret associations; but it was none the less efficacious and binding. As the members of a clan regarded themselves as brothers and sisters, marriages among them were not allowed. This led, of course, to constant intermarriages between members of the different clans of which a nation was composed, thus binding the whole nation together. What the founders of the Iroquois League did was to extend this system of social alliances through the entire confederacy. The Wolf clansman of the Caniengas was deemed a brother of the Wolf clansman of the Senecas, though originally there may have been no special connection between them. It was a tie apparently artificial in its origin, as much so as the tie which binds a freemason of Berlin to a freemason of New Orleans. But it came to have all the strength of a tie of kindred. Mr. Morgan has well pointed out the

---

[1] Ancient Society, p. 163.
[2] Ibid, p. 168.
[3] Rotisennakete, and Rotinenhiotronon. See J. A. Cuoq, Lexique de la Langue Iroquoise, p. 154. The proper meaning of these names will be hereafter shown.
[4] League of the Iroquois, p. 91.

wisdom shown by the Iroquois founders, in availing themselves of this powerful element of strength in the formation of their federal constitution. [1] Their government, though politically a league of nations, was socially a combination of clans. In this way Hiawatha and Dekanawidah may be deemed to have given to the system of clanship an extension and a force which it had not previously possessed; and it is by no means unlikely that this example may, as the Iroquois assert, have acted upon neighboring nations, and led to a gradual increase in the number and influence of these brotherhoods.

But here a discrepancy presents itself in the Iroquois system, which has perplexed all who have written on the subject. Two of the Six Nations, the Caniengas and Oneidas, had only three clans, the Wolf, the Tortoise and the Bear; while the others had, or at least have, each eight or nine, and these variously styled in the different nations. The three which have been named are, indeed, found in all; but besides these three, the Onondagas have five, Deer, Eel, Beaver, Ball and Snipe. The Cayugas and Senecas have also eight clans, which are similar to those of the Onondagas, except that among the Cayugas the Ball clan is replaced by the Hawk, and among the Senecas both Ball and Eel disappear, and are replaced by Hawk and Heron. The Tuscaroras have likewise eight clans, but among these are neither the Hawk, the Heron or the Ball. In lieu of them the Wolf clan is divided into two, the Gray Wolf and the Yellow Wolf, and the Tortoise furnishes two, the Great Tortoise and the Little Tortoise; [2] the Bear, the Beaver, the Eel and the Snipe remain, as among the Onondagas, Cayugas and Senecas.

We are naturally led to ask how it happens that only three clans are found among the Caniengas and Oneidas, while the other nations have eight. Mr. Morgan was inclined to think that the other five once existed among the

---

[1] League of the Iroquois, p. 82, et seq.

[2] It is deserving of notice that this division of the Tortoise clan seems to p. 54 exist in a nascent form among the Onondagas. The name of this clan is Hahnowa, which is the general word for tortoise; but the clan is divided into two septs or subdivisions, the Hanyatengona, or Great Tortoise, and the Nikahnowaksa, or Little Tortoise, which together are held to constitute but one clan. How or why the distinction is kept up I did not learn. In the Book of Rites the Tortoise clan is also spoken of in the dual number--"the two clans of the Tortoise." it is probable, therefore, that this partial subdivision extended throughout the original Five Nations, and became complete among the Tuscaroras.

two former nations, and had become extinct. [1] The native annalists of those nations, however, affirm that no more than three clans ever existed among them. This assertion is now confirmed, indirectly but strongly, by the testimony of the Book of Rites, which seems to show that only three clans were recognized in the whole confederacy when the League was formed. All the towns of the united nations were distributed among the three primary clans of the Wolf, the Tortoise and the Bear. If the other clans existed, it was probably merely as septs or divisions of these three. [2] It is more likely, however, that these additional clans were of later creation or introduction. Their origin, as well as their restriction to the three western nations, may be easily explained. The successive conquests achieved by the Iroquois in the early part of the seventeenth century had the result of incorporating with their people great numbers of Hurons, Eries, Attiwandaronks, Andastes, and other captives belonging to tribes of the same stock, speaking similar dialects, and having usages closely resembling those of their captors. Of these captives, some were directly adopted into the Iroquois families and clans; but a larger number remained for a time in separate towns, retaining their own usages. They were regarded, however, and they regarded themselves, as Iroquois. Constant intercourse and frequent intermarriages soon abolished all distinctions of national origin. But the distinction of clanship would remain. The Hurons (or, at least, the Tionontates, or Tobacco Nation) had clans of the Deer and the Hawk, and they had a Snake clan bearing a name (yagontrunon) not unlike the name of the Onondaga Eel clan (ogontena), and evidently derived from the same root. The other conquered nations had doubtless some peculiar clans; for these brotherhoods, as has been shown, were constantly in process of formation and change among the Indian tribes. Almost all the captives were incorporated with the three western nations of the League, to whom the conquered tribes were mostly nearer than to

---

[1] League of the Iroquois, p. 81. Ancient Society, p. 92.
[2] "The Turtle family, or the Anowara, was the most noble of the whole League; next came the Ochquari, or clan of the Bear, and the Oquacho, or that of the Wolf. These three were so prominent that Zeisberger hardly recognizes the others."--De Sehweinitz's Life of Zeisberger, p. 79. Zeisberger had been adopted into the nation of the Onondagas and the clan of the Tortoise. His knowledge of the laws and usages of the Kanonsionni was acquired chiefly in that nation. Charlevoix makes the Bear the leading clan of the Iroquois. It would seem that the relative rank of the clans varied in the different nations. The chiefs of the Wolf clan come first in the list of Oneida councillors.

the Caniengas and Oneidas. The origin of the additional clans among the Onondagas, Cayugas and Senecas is thus readily understood.

One fact, important in its connection with the structure of the federal council, remains to be noted, and if possible, elucidated. The councillors of each nation were divided into classes, whose part in the deliberations of the councils bore a certain resemblance to that held by the committees of our legislatures. The operation of this system cannot be better described than in the words of Morgan: "The founders of the confederacy, seeking to obviate, as far as possible, altercation in council, and to facilitate their progress to unanimity, divided the sachems of each nation into classes, usually of two or three each, as will be seen by referring to the table of sachemships. No sachem was permitted to express an opinion in council, until he had agreed with the other sachem or sachems of his class upon the opinion to be expressed, and had received an appointment to act as speaker for the class. Thus the eight Seneca sachems, being in four classes, could have but four opinions, the ten Cayuga sachems but four. In this manner each class was brought to unanimity within itself. A cross-consultation was then held between the four sachems who represented the four classes; and when they had agreed, they appointed one of their number to express their resulting opinion, which was the answer of their nation. The several nations having, by this ingenious method, become of "one mind" separately, it only remained to compare their several opinions to arrive at the final sentiment of all the sachems of the League. This was effected by a conference between the individual representatives of the several nations; and when they had arrived at unanimity, the answer of the League was determined." [1]

A careful consideration of the facts, in the light cast upon them by the evidence of the "Book of Rites" and the testimony of the Canadian Iroquois, leaves no doubt that these classes were originally identical with the clans. Among the Caniengas and Oneidas this identity still exists. Each of these nations received nine representatives in the federal council. These were-- and still are--divided into three classes, each composed of three members, and each class representing a clan. In the Canienga tribe the members of the first class are all of the Tortoise clan, those of the second class are of the Wolf clan, and those of the third class of the Bear clan. Among the Oneidas, the councillors of the first class belong to the Wolf clan, those of

---

[1] League of the Iroquois, p, 112.

the second class to the Tortoise clan, and those of the third class to the Bear clan. Such was the information which Mr. Morgan received from his Seneca friends and such I found to be the fact among the Iroquois now in Canada. When we come to the other nations we find a wholly different state of things. No correspondence now exists between the classes and the clans. The Cayugas have now, as has been shown, eight clans; but of these only six, according to the list given by Morgan, and only five in that furnished to me by the Canadian chiefs, are represented in the council. These are distributed in three classes, which do not correspond to the clans. In Morgan's list the first class has five members, the first of whom belongs to the Deer clan, the second to that of the Heron, the third and fourth to that of the Bear, and the fifth to that of the Tortoise. In my list this class also comprises five chiefs, of whom the first two (identical in name with the first two of Morgan) belong to the Deer clan, while the third (who bears the same name as Mr. Morgan's third) is of the Bear clan. In the "Book of Rites" the first Cayuga class comprises only two chiefs, but their clans (which were supposed to be known to the hearers) are not indicated. The fourteen Onondaga councillors are divided into five classes, according to Morgan, and also in the modern Canadian list. The "Book of Rites" seems to give only four, but none of these--according to the evidence of the Canadian chiefs--correspond with the modern clans; and the same councillor, in lists received from different sources, is found to belong to different classes and different clans. Thus the distinguished title of Skanawati is borne, in Mr. Morgan's list, by a chief of the fifth class and of the third clan. In the list obtained by me at Onondaga Castle this chief is of the fourth class and of the Ball clan. The great Seneca chief Kanyadariyo is, in Mr. Morgan's list, a member of the Tortoise clan, while among the Canadian Senecas he belongs to the Wolf clan. In short, it is evident that the introduction of the new clans among the western nations has thrown this part of their constitutional system into confusion. The probability is that when the confederacy was established only three clans, Bear, Wolf and Tortoise, existed among the Iroquois, as only three clans, Bear, Wolf and Turkey, existed in recent times among their Algonkin neighbors, the Lenni Lenape, or Delawares. Thus the classes of their Council grew spontaneously out of their clan system, as the senators of each clan would naturally consult together. Afterwards new clans arose; but it seems probable that when the list of councillors comprised in the "Book of Rites" was written--that is, about the middle of the last century--the correspondence of classes and clans was still maintained. The number of both was increased in the western tribes, but each class was still composed of chiefs of the same clan. The written book fixed the classes to a certain extent, but the clans to which their members belonged continued to vary, under the influence of political and social changes. If, at the death of a councillor, no member of his clan was found qualified to succeed him, a successor would be elected from another clan which was deemed to be in some way connected with him. I was assured by the Onondaga chiefs of the New York Reservation that this was their rule at present; and it is quite sufficient to account for the departure, in the western nations, from the ancient system. It is evident that after the nations and clans were rent to fragments by the dissensions and emigration caused by the American Revolution, these changes would, for a time, be necessarily frequent. And thus it happens that chiefs are found in the duplicate confederacies which after this disruption were established in Canada and New York, who bear the same titular designation, but differ both in the clans and in the classes to which they belong.

THE CONDOLENCE AND THE INSTALLATION

WITH the arrival at the Council House the "opening ceremony" is concluded. In the house the members of the Council were seated in the usual array, on opposite sides of the house. On one side were the three elder nations, the Caniengas, Onondagas, and Senecas, and on the other the younger, who were deemed, and styled in Council, the offspring of the former. These younger members, originally two in number, the Oneidas and Cayugas, had afterwards an important accession in the Tuscarora nation; and in later years several smaller tribes, or, as they were styled, additional braces of the Extended House, were received,-- Tuteloes, Nanticokes, Delawares and others. In the Onondaga portion of the book the younger tribes speak as "we three brothers." The earliest of the later accessions seems to have taken place about the year 1753, when the Tuteloes and Nanticokes were admitted.[1] These circumstances afford additional evidence that the Book was originally written prior to that date and subsequent to the year 1714, when the Tuscaroras were received into the League.

If the deceased chief belonged to one of the three older nations, the duty of conducting the condoling ceremony which followed was performed by the younger nations, who mourned for him as for a father or an uncle. If he were a chief of one of the younger nations, the others lamented him as a son or a nephew. The mourning nations selected as their representative a high chief, usually a distinguished orator, familiar with the usages and laws of the League, to conduct these ceremonies. The lamentations followed a prescribed routine, each successive topic of condolence being indicated by a string of wampum, which, by the arrangement of its beads, recalled the words to the memory of the officiating chief. In the "Book of Rites" we have these addresses of condolence in a twofold form. The Canienga book gives us the form used by the elder nations; and the Onondaga supplement adds the form employed by the younger brothers. The former is more ancient, and apparently more dignified and formal. The speaker addresses the mourners as his children (konyennetaghkwen, "my offspring,") and

---

[1] N.Y. Hist. Col., Vol. 6, p. 811. Stone's Life of Sir William Johnson, p. 414.

recites each commonplace of condolence in a curt and perfunctory style. He wipes away their tears that they may see clearly; he opens their ears that they may hear readily. He removes from their throats the obstruction with which their grief is choking them, so that they may ease their burdened minds by speaking freely to their friends. And finally, as the loss of their lamented chief may have occurred in war--and at all events many of their friends have thus perished--he cleans the mats on which they are sitting from the figurative bloodstains, so that they may for a time cease to be reminded of their losses, and may regain their former cheerfulness.

The condolence of the younger brothers, expressed in the Onondaga book, is more expansive and more sympathetic. Though apparently disfigured and mutilated by repeated transcriptions, it bears marks of having been originally the composition of a superior mind. All such topics of consolation as would occur to a speaker ignorant or regardless of a future life are skillfully presented, and the. whole address is imbued with a sentiment of cordial tenderness and affection. Those who have been accustomed to regard the Indians as a cold-hearted people will find it difficult to reconcile that view of their character with the contrary evidence afforded by this genuine expression of their feelings, and, indeed, by the whole tenor of the Book.

This address concludes with the emphatic words, "I have finished; now point me the man;" or, as the words were paraphrased by the interpreter, "Now show me the warrior who is to be the new chief." The candidate for senatorial honors, who is to take the place and name of the deceased councillor, is then brought forward by his nation. His admission by the assembled Council, at this stage of the proceedings, is a matter of course; for his nation had taken care to ascertain, before the meeting, that the object of their choice would be acceptable to the councillors of the other nations. The ceremony of induction consisted in the formal bestowal of the new name by which he was henceforth to be known. A chief placed himself on each side of the candidate, and, grasping his arms, marched him to and fro in the Council house, between the lines of the assembled senators. As they walked they proclaimed his new name and office, and recited, in a measured chant, the duties to which he was now called, the audience responding at every pause with the usual chorus of assent.

When this ceremony was finished, and the new councillor had taken his proper seat among the nobles of his nation, the wampum belts, which

The Iroquois Book of Rites

comprised the historical records of the federation, were produced, and the officiating chief proceeded to explain them, one by one, to the assemblage. This was called "reading the archives." In this way a knowledge of the events signified by the wampum was fastened, by repeated iteration, in the minds of the listeners. Those who doubt whether events which occurred four centuries ago can be remembered as clearly and minutely as they are now recited, will probably have their doubts removed when, they consider the necessary operation of this custom. The orator's narrative is repeated in the presence of many auditors who have often heard it before, and who would be prompt to remark and to correct any departure from the well-known history.

This narrative is not recorded in the Book of Rites. At the time when that was written, the annals of the confederacy were doubtless supposed to be sufficiently preserved by the wampum records. The speeches and ceremonies which followed, and which were of equal, if not greater importance, had no such evidences to recall them. From this statement, however, the "hymn" should be excepted; to each line of it, except the last, a wampum string was devoted. With this exception, all was left to the memory of the orator. The Homeric poems, the hymns of the Vedas, the Kalewala, the Polynesian genealogies, and many other examples, show the exactness with which a composition that interests a whole nation may be handed down; but it is not surprising that when the chiefs became aware of the superior advantages of a written record, they should have had recourse to it. We need not doubt that Chief David of Schoharie, or whoever else was the scribe appointed to this duty, has faithfully preserved the substance, and, for the most part, the very words, of the speeches and chants which he had often heard under such impressive circumstances.

The hymn, or karenna, deserves a special notice. In every important council of the Iroquois a song or chant is considered a proper and almost essential part of the proceedings. Such official songs are mentioned in many reports of treaty councils held with them by the French and English authorities. In this greatest of all councils the song must, of course, have a distinguished place. It follows immediately upon the address of greeting and condolence, and is, in fact, regarded as the completion of it, and the introduction to the equally important ceremony which is to follow, viz., the repetition of the ancient laws of the confederacy. This particular hymn is of great antiquity. Some of the chiefs expressed to me the opinion that it was composed by Dekanawidah or Hiawatha. Its tenor, however, as well as that of the whole book, shows that it belongs to a later period. The ceremonies of the council were doubtless prescribed by the founders of the League; but the speeches of the Book, and this hymn, all refer to the League as the work of a past age. The speakers appeal to the wisdom of their forefathers (literally, their grandsires), and lament the degeneracy of the later times. They expressly declare that those who established the "great peace" were in their graves, and had taken their work with them and placed it as a pillow under them. This is the language of men who remembered the founders, and to whom the burial of the last of them was a comparatively recent event. If the League was formed, as seems probable, about the year 1450, the speeches and hymn, in their present form, may reasonably be referred to the early part of the next century. There is reason to believe that the formation of the confederacy was followed by wars with the Hurons and Algonkin tribes, in which, as usual, many changes of fortune took place. If the Hurons, as has been shown, were expelled from their abode on the northern shore of the St. Lawrence, the Mohegans, on the other hand, inflicted some serious blows upon the eastern nations of the confederacy.[1] The Delawares were not conquered and reduced to subjection without a long and sanguinary struggle. In a Condoling Council we might expect that the tone of feeling would be lugubrious; but the sense of loss and of danger is too marked in all the speeches of the Canienga Book to be merely a formal utterance. It does not appear in those of the Onondaga Book, which is seemingly of later composition.

The "karenna," or chant of the Condoling Council, may be styled the National Hymn of the Iroquois. A comparison between it and other national hymns, whose chief characteristics are self-glorification and defiance, might afford room for some instructive inferences. This hymn, it should be remarked, brief as it is, is regarded by the Indians as a collection of songs. Each line, in fact, is, in their view, a song by itself, and is brought to mind by its own special wampum string, In singing, each line is twice repeated, and is introduced and followed by many long-drawn repetitions of the exclamation aihaigh (or rather haihaih) which is rendered "hail!" and from which the hymn derives its designation. In the first line the speaker salutes the "Peace," or the league, whose blessings they enjoy. In the next he greets the kindred of the deceased chief, who are the special objects of the public sympathy. Then he salutes the oyenkondonh, a term which has been rendered "warriors." This rendering, however, may have a misleading

---

[1] See the Jesuit Relation for 1660, p. 6.

effect. The word has nothing to do with war, unless in the sense that every grown man in an Indian community is supposed to be a soldier. Except in this hymn, the word in question is now disused. An elderly chief assured me that he had sung it for years without knowing its precise meaning. Some of his fellow-councillors were better informed. The word is apparently derived from onkwe, man, which in the Onondaga dialect becomes yenkwe. It comprises all the men (the "manhood" or mankind) of the nation--as, in the following verse, the word wakonnyh, which is also obsolete, signifies the "womanhood," or all the women of the people with whom the singer condoles. In the next line he invokes the laws which their forefathers established; and he concludes by calling upon his hearers to listen to the wisdom of their forefathers, which he is about to recite. As a whole, the hymn may be described as an expression of reverence for the laws and for the dead, and of sympathy with the living. Such is the "national anthem,"--the Marseillaise,---of the ferocious Iroquois.

The regard for women which is apparent in this hymn, and in other passages of the Book, is deserving of notice. The common notion that women among the Indians were treated as inferiors, and made "beasts of burden," is unfounded so far as the Iroquois are concerned, and among all other tribes of which I have any knowledge. With them, as with civilized nations, the work of the community and the cares of the family are fairly divided. Among the Iroquois the hunting and fishing, the house-building and canoe-making, fell to the men. The women cooked, made the dresses, scratched the ground with their light hoes, planted and gathered the crops, and took care of the children. The household goods belonged to the woman. On her death, her relatives, and not her husband, claimed them. The children were also hers; they belonged to her clan, and in case of a separation they went with her. She was really the head of the household; and in this capacity her right, when she chanced to be the oldest matron of a noble family, to select the successor of a deceased chief of that family, was recognized by the highest law of the confederacy. That this rank and position were greatly prized is shown by a remarkable passage in the Jesuit Relations. A Canienga matron, becoming a Christian, left her country, with two of her children, to enjoy greater freedom in her devotions among the French. The act, writes the missionary, so offended her family that, in a public meeting of the town, "they degraded her from the rank of the nobility, and took from her the title of Oyander, that is, honorable (considérable)--a title which they esteem highly, and which she had inherited from her ancestors, and deserved by her good judgment, her prudence, and her excellent conduct and at the same time they installed another in her place." [1]

The complete equality of the sexes in social estimation and influence is apparent in all the narratives of the early missionaries, who were the best possible judges on this point. Casual observers have been misled by the absence of those artificial expressions of courtesy which have descended to us from the time of chivalry, and which, however gracious and pleasing to witness, are, after all, merely signs of condescension and protection from the strong to the weak. The Iroquois does not give up his seat to a woman, or yield her precedence on leaving a room; but he secures her in the possession of her property, he recognizes her right to the children she has borne, and he submits to her decision the choice of his future rulers.

---

[1] Relation of 1671, p. 6. The word oyander in modern pronunciation becomes oyaner. It is derived from the root yaner, noble, and is the feminine form of the word royaner, lord, or nobleman,---the title applied to the members of the federal council.

THE LAWS OF THE LEAGUE

IT is the custom of the officiating orator, while the chant is going on, to walk to and fro in the council-house. When the hymn is finished, he breaks out into a passionate invocation to their forefathers, and a lament over the degeneracy of the times. This, as the French missionaries inform us, was a favorite topic of Indian speakers.[1] Among the Iroquois, who could look back to an era of genuine statesmen and heroes, the authors of their constitution, this complaint must have had a peculiar force and Sincerity. After this appeal to the founders of their state, there naturally followed an address to the Council and the people, reciting "all the rules they decided on, which they thought would strengthen the house." By "the house" was meant, of course, the house of many hearths, to which they likened their confederacy. The "rules" or laws which follow require some explanation, that their full value may be understood.

The first law prescribes that when a chief dies his office shall not perish with him. This is expressed, in their metaphorical style, by an injunction that the "horns," or insignia of office, shall not be buried with the deceased chief, but shall be taken off at his death, to be transferred to his successor. This rule is laid down in the most urgent and impressive terms. "We should perhaps all perish if his office is buried with him in his grave." This systematic transmission of official rank was, in fact, the vital principle of their government. It was in this system that their federal union differed from the frequent and transitory confederacies common among the Indian tribes. In general, among nearly all the tribes, the rank of a chief was personal. It was gained by the character and achievements of the individual, and it died with him. Hence their government and policy, so far as they can be said to have had any, were always uncertain and fluctuating. No person understood the Indian usages better than Zeisberger. His biographer has well described the difference which existed in this respect between the Iroquois and their neighbors. "The Algonkins," he writes, "knew nothing of regular government. They had no system of polity; there was no unity of

---

[1] See the Relation of 1639, p. 57: "C'est la plainte ordinaire des Capitaines [of the Hurons] que tout se va perdant, à faute de garder les formes et coustoumes de leurs ancestres."

action among them. The affairs even of a single tribe were managed in the loosest manner." After briefly, but accurately, delineating the Iroquois system of councils, he adds: "Thus they became both a political and a military power among the aborigines; the influence of their league was felt everywhere, and their conquests extended in every direction."[1] The principle that "the chief dies but the office survives,"--the regular transmission of rank, title and authority, by a method partly hereditary and partly elective,---was the principle on which the life and strength of the Iroquois constitution depended.

Next followed a provision of hardly less importance. The wars among the Indian tribes arise almost always from individual murders. The killing of a tribesman by the members of another community concerns his whole people. If satisfaction is not promptly made, war follows, as a matter of course.[2] The founders of the Iroquois commonwealth decreed that wars for this cause should not be allowed to rise between any of their cantons. On this point a special charge was given to the members of the Great Council. They were enjoined (in the figurative language employed throughout the Book) not to allow the murder to be discussed in a national assembly, where the exasperation of the young men might lead to mischief, but to reserve it for their own consideration; and they were required as soon as possible to bury all animosities that might arise from it. The figure employed is impressive. They were to uproot a huge pine-tree-- the well-known emblem of their League--disclosing a deep cavity, below which an underground stream would be swiftly flowing. Into this current they were to cast the cause of trouble, and then, replacing the tree, hide the mischief forever from their people.

How strictly in spirit these injunctions were followed, and with what good effect, their whole history shows. A notable instance of the readiness and ingenuity of their statesmen in finding the means of public reconciliation in such cases is given in the Jesuit narrative. On the 24th of July, 1657, a great council was held at Onondaga to consider three matters, all of special import. First in order was the necessity of appeasing a threatened quarrel

---

[1] De Schweinitz: Life of Zeisberger, p. 39.
[2] Relation, of 1636, p. 119. "C'est de la que naissent les guerres, et c'est un sujet plus que suffisant deprendre les armes contre quelque Village quand il refuse de satisfaire par les presents ordonnez, pour celuy qui vous aurait tué quelq'un des vostres."--Brebeuf, on the Hurons.

between two of the leading nations, the Senecas and the Caniengas, caused by a misadventure in which a Seneca "captain" had been killed by some warriors of the eastern nation. Next in importance was the reception of a large party of Frenchmen, headed by Father Francis le Mercier, the Superior of the Jesuit missionaries in Canada, who had come to form a settlement among the Iroquois. And, finally, they had to prepare the plan and the means for an expedition against some hostile tribes. Before the meeting of the Council the Frenchmen had paid a formal visit to the Seneca delegates, whom they found "filling the air with songs of mourning" for their slaughtered chief, and had manifested their sympathy by a present, "to alleviate the grief" of the mourners. This incident seems to have suggested to the assembled councillors a method of effecting --or at least of announcing--the desired accommodation, and of paying at the same time a happy compliment to their reverend visitors. By common consent the affair was referred to the arbitrament of the Father Superior, by whom the difference was promptly settled. [1] It was not necessary for the politic senators to inform their gratified visitors that the performance in which they thus took part was merely a formality which ratified, or rather proclaimed, a foregone conclusion. The reconciliation which was prescribed by their constitution had undoubtedly been arranged by previous conferences, after their custom in such matters, before the meeting of the Council. [2] So effective was this provision of their constitution that for more than three centuries this main cause of Indian wars was rendered innocuous, and the "Great Peace" remained undisturbed. This proud averment of their annalists, confirmed as it is for more than half the period by the evidence of their white neighbors, cannot reasonably be questioned. What nation or confederacy of civilized Europe can show an exemption from domestic strife for so long a term?

---

[1] "On tint ce grand conseil le 24 du mois de Juillet, où toutes les Nations remisent entre les mains d'Achiendase (qui est nostre Père Superieur) le differend d'entre les Sonnontoüeronnons et les Agnieronnons, qui fut bientot terminé."--Relation of 1657, p. 16.

[2] For a curious instance of the manner in which questions to be apparently decided by a Council were previously settled between the parties, see the Life of Zeisberger, p. 190: "Gietterowane was the speaker on one side, Zeisberger on the other. These two consulted together privately,---Zeisberger unfolding the import of the strings [of wampum which he had brought as ambassador] and Gietterowane committing to memory what he said."

The third rule or ordinance which the founders enacted "to strengthen the house" is of a remarkable character. It relates to the mortuary usages of the people; and when these are understood, the great importance of this law becomes apparent. Among the Indians of the Huron-Iroquois family the ordinary mourning for the dead became exaggerated into customs of the most extravagant character, exhausting the time and strength of the warriors, and devouring their substance. The French missionaries have left us an account of these singular usages among the Hurons, some of which excited their respect, and others their astonishment. "Our savages," they wrote, "are in no way savage as regards the duties which nature herself requires us to render to the dead. You would say that their efforts, their toils and their commerce had no other end than to amass the means of honoring the departed. They have nothing too precious for this object. To this they devote their robes of skins, their hatchets and wampum, in such profusion that you would fancy they made nothing of them; and yet these are the riches of their country. Often in midwinter you will see them going almost naked, while they have at home, laid up in store, good and handsome robes, which they keep in reverence for the dead. This is their point of honor. In this, above all, they seek to show themselves magnificent." [1]

During the three days that preceded the burial of the dead, or the removal of his remains to the scaffold, the wails, groans and lamentations of the relatives and neighbors resounded in the cabin where he lay. All the stored riches were brought forth and lavished in gifts "to comfort the mourners." The mourning did not end with the burial; in fact, it may be said to have then only begun. The "great mourning," as the missionaries term it, lasted for six days longer, during which the mourners lay, face downward, upon their mats, and enveloped in their robes, speechless, or replying only by an ejaculation to those who addressed them. During this period they had no fire in the house, even in winter; they ate their food cold, and left the cabin only at night, and as secretly as possible. The "lesser mourning" lasted for a year, during which they refrained from oiling their hair, attended public festivals rarely, and only (in the case of women) when their mothers ordered, and were forbidden to marry again.

This, however, was not all. Once in twelve years was held a great ceremony of reinterment,---a solemn "feast of the dead," as it was called. Until the

---

[1] Brebeuf, Relation of 1636, p. 128.

day of this feast arrived, funeral rites in honor of the departed were repeated from time to time, and feasts were held, at which, as the expression was, their names were revived, while presents were distributed, as at the time of their death. The great Feast of the Dead, however, was the most important of all their ceremonies. The bodies of all who had died in the nation during the preceding twelve years were then exhumed, or removed from the scaffolds on which they had been laid, and the festering corpses or cleansed bones were all interred together in a vast pit lined with robes of beaver skins, the most precious of all their furs. Wampum, copper implements, earthenware, the most valued of their possessions, were cast into the pit, which was then solemnly closed with earth. While the ceremony was going on, rich presents of all descriptions, the accumulations of the past twelve years, were distributed by the relatives of the deceased among the people. In this distribution, strange to say, valuable fur robes were frequently cut and torn to pieces, so as to be rendered worthless. A lavish display and reckless destruction of wealth were deemed honors due to the shades of the departed. [1]

The Attiwandaronks, or Neutrals, who were the nearest neighbors of the Iroquois, were still more extravagant in their demonstrations of affection for their lost friends. They, too, had their feasts of the dead, at regular intervals. In the meantime the bodies were kept in their houses as long as possible--"until the stench became intolerable." Then, when this proximity could no longer be borne, the remains were left for a period to decay on a scaffold in the open air. After a time the remaining flesh was removed from the bones, which were arranged on the sides of their cabins, in full view of the inmates, until the great day of general interment. With these mournful objects before their eyes, renewing constantly the sense of their loss, the women of the household were excited to frequent outbursts of grief, expressed in wailing chants. [2]

---

[1] See the Relation for 1636, p. 131. A most vivid and graphic. description of these extraordinary ceremonies is given in Parkman's admirable work, The Jesuits in North America, Chapter 7.

[2] "Cet object qu'ils ont devant les yeux, leur renouvellant continuellement le resentiment de leurs pertes, leur fait ordinairement ietter des cris, et faire des lamentations tout à fait lugubres, le tout en chanson. Mais cela ne se fait que par les femmes."--Relation of 1641, p. 73.

That the Iroquois in ancient times had funeral customs similar to those of their sister nations, and not less revolting, cannot be doubted. How these shocking and pernicious usages were abolished at one swoop is shown by the brief passage in the Book of Rites now under discussion. The injunctions are laconic, but full of meaning. When a death occurs, the people are told, "this shall be done." A delegation of persons, officially appointed for the purpose, shall repair to the dwelling of the deceased, bearing in a pouch some strands of mourning wampum. The leader, holding these strands, and standing by the hearth, shall address, in the name of the whole people, a few words of comfort to the mourners. And then "they shall be comforted," and shall go on with their usual duties. To this simple ceremony--supplemented, in the case of a high chief, by the rites of the "Condoling Council,"--the preposterous funeral usages, which pervaded the lives and wasted the wealth of the other nations of this stock, were reduced, by the wisdom of the Iroquois legislators.

In considering these remarkable laws, it becomes evident that the work which Hiawatha and Dekanawidah accomplished was really a Great Reformation, not merely political, but also social and religious. They desired not only to establish peace among the nations, but also to abolish or modify such usages and beliefs as in their opinion were injurious to their people. It is deserving of notice that a divinity unknown, at least in name, to the Hurons, received special reverence among the Iroquois. The chief characters of the Huron pantheon were a female deity, Ataensic, a sort of Hecate, whom they sometimes identified with the moon, and her grandson, Juskeha, who was sometimes regarded as the sun, and as a benevolent spirit, but most commonly in their stories appears as a fantastic and capricious goblin, with no moral attributes whatever. In the Iroquois mythology these deities are replaced by a personage of a much higher character. Taronhiawagon, the Holder of the Heavens, was with them the Master of Life. He declared his will to them in dreams, and in like manner disclosed future events, particularly such as were important to the public welfare. He was, in fact, the national god of the Iroquois. It was he who guided their fathers in their early wanderings, when they were seeking for a place of abode. He visited them from time to time, in person, to protect them from their enemies and to instruct them in useful arts.

It is possible that the Iroquois Taronhiawagon may have been originally the same as the Huron Juskeha. Some eminent authorities on Indian mythology are inclined to this opinion. On the other hand, the earlier Jesuit missionaries give no hint of such identity, and the Tuscarora historian, Cusick, seems to distinguish between these divine personages. But whether we accept this view or seek for any other origin, there seems reason to suppose that the more exalted conception of this deity, who is certainly, in character and attributes, one of the noblest creations of the North American mythologies, dates from the era of the confederacy, when he became more especially the chief divinity and protector of the Kanonsionni. [1]

---

[1] See for Taronhiawagon the Jesuit Relations for 1670, pp. 47, 66, and for 1671, p. 17: also Cusick, pp. 20, 22, 24, 34. For Juskeha, see the Relation for 1635, p. 34; 1636, pp. 101-103; 1640, p. 92. Lafitau in one place makes Tharonhiawagon a deified man, and in another the grandson of Ataensic.--Mœurs des Sauvages Ameriquains, Vol. I, p. 146 and p. 244.

HISTORICAL TRADITIONS

AFTER the declaration of the laws of the League, there follows a passage of great historical importance. The speaker recites the names of the chiefs who represented the Five Nations in the conference by which the work of devising their laws and establishing their government was accomplished. The native name of the confederacy is here for the first time mentioned. In the guttural and rather irregular orthography of the Book it is spelt Kanonghsyonny. The Roman Catholic missionaries, neglecting the aspirate, which in the Iroquois pronunciation appears and disappears as capriciously as in the spoken dialects of the south of England, write the word Kanonsionni. It is usually rendered by interpreters the "Long House," but this is not precisely its meaning. The ordinary word for "long house" is kanonses or kanonsis, the termination es or is being the adjective suffix which signifies long. Kanonsionni is a compound word, formed of kanonsa, house, and ionni, extended, or drawn out. The confederacy was compared to a dwelling which was extended by additions made to the end, in the manner in which their bark-built houses were lengthened,---sometimes to an extent exceeding two hundred feet. When the number of families inhabiting these long dwellings was increased by marriage or adoption, and a new hearth was required, the end-wall,---if this term may be applied to the slight frame of poles and bark which closed the house,---was removed, an addition of the required size was made to the edifice, and the closing wall was restored. Such was the figure by which the founders of the confederacy represented their political structure, a figure which was in itself a description and an invitation. It declared that the united nations were not distinct tribes, associated by a temporary league, but one great family, clustered for convenience about separate hearths in a common dwelling; and it proclaimed their readiness to receive new members into the general household. [1]

---

[1] The people of the confederacy were known as Rotinoñsioñni,---They of the Extended House." In the Seneca dialect this was altered and abridged to Hotinoñsoñni, the ñ having the French nasal sound. This word is written by Mr. Morgan, "Hodenosaunee."

The Iroquois Book of Rites 57

The names of the six great chiefs who, as representatives of their several nations, formed the confederacy, are in this narrative linked together in a manner which declares their political kinship. The first rulers or heads of the combined households were the Canienga Dekanawidah with his "joint-ruler" and political son, the Oneida Otatsehte (or Odadsheghte), whose union with Dekanawidah was the commencement of the League. Next follows Otatsehte's uncle (and Dekanawidah's brother), the Onondaga Wathadodarho (Atotarho), who is accompanied by his son, the Cayuga Akahenyonh. The uncle of the Cayuga representative, the Seneca chief Kanadariyu, and his cousin, Shadekaronyes, represent the two sections into which the great Seneca nation was divided. The name of Hiawatha does not appear in this enumeration. According to the uniform tradition of the Five Nations, he was not merely present in the convention, but was the leading spirit in its deliberations. But he did not officially represent any nation. By birth a high chief of the Onondagas, he had been but newly adopted among the Caniengas. Each of these nations had entrusted its interests to its own most influential chief. But the respect with which Hiawatha was regarded is indicated, as has been already remarked, by his place in the list of fifty councillors, with whose names the Book concludes. Though so recently received among the haughty Caniengas, whose proud and jealous temper is often noticed by the missionaries and other early observers, his name is placed second in the list of their representatives, immediately following that of Tekarihoken, the chief who stood highest in titular rank among the nobles of the Kanonsionni, and whose lineage was perhaps derived from the leader of their primitive migrations.

The tradition runs that when the political frame of their confederacy had been arranged by the members of this convention, and the number of senators who should represent each nation in the federal council had been determined, the six delegates, with Hiawatha and some other advisers, went through all the nations, selecting--doubtless with the aid of a national council in each case--the chiefs who were to constitute the first council. In designating these,---or rather, probably, in the ceremonies of their installation,---it is said that some peculiar prerogative was conceded to the Onondagas,---that is, to Atotarho and his attendant chiefs. It was probably given as a mark of respect, rather than as conferring any real authority; but from this circumstance the Onondagas were afterwards known in the council by the title of "the nominators." The word is, in the Canienga dialect, Rotisennakehte,---in Onondaga, Hotisennakehte. It means literally, "the name-carriers,"--as if, said one of my informants, they bore a parcel of names in a bag slung upon the back.

Each of the other nations had also its peculiar name in the Council, distinct from the mere local designation by which it was commonly called. Thus the Caniengas had for their "Council name" the term Tehadirihoken. This is the plural form of the name of their leading chief, Tekarihoken. Opinions differ much among the Indians as to the meaning of this name. Cusick, the Tuscarora historian, defines it "a speech divided," and apparently refers it to the division of the Iroquois language into dialects. Chief George Johnson, the interpreter, rendered it "two statements together," or "two pieces of news together." Another native informant thought it meant "one-word in two divisions," while a third defined it as meaning "between two words." The root-word of the name is the Canienga orihwa, or karihwa (properly karihöa), which is defined "thing, affair, speech, news." [1] It also apparently means office; thus we have the derivatives garihont, "to give some charge or duty to some one," and atrihont, "to be an officer, or captain." The name is in the peculiar dual or rather duplicative form which is indicated by the prefix te and the affix ken or ke. It may possibly, therefore, mean "holding two offices," and would thus be specially applicable to the great Canienga noble, who, unlike most of his order, was both a civil ruler and a war-chief. But whether he gave his name to his people, or received it from them, is uncertain. In other instances the Council name of a nation appears to have been applied in the singular number to the leading chief of the nation. Thus the head-chief of the Onondagas was often known by the title of Sakosen-nakehte, "the Name-carrier." [2]

The name of the Oneida nation in the Council was Nihatirontakowa--or, in the Onondaga dialect, Nihatientakona--usually rendered the "Great-Tree People,"--literally, "those of the great log." It is derived from karonta, a fallen tree, or piece of timber, with the suffix kowa or kona, great, added, and the verb-forming pronoun prefixed. In the singular number it becomes Niharontakowa, which would be understood to mean "He is an Oneida."

---

[1] See Bruyas, sub voce Garihöa. Mr. Morgan (League of the Iroquois, p. 97), who derived his information from the Senecas, says that the name "was a term of respect, and signifies 'neutral,' or, as it may be rendered, the shield." He adds, "its origin is lost in obscurity."

[2] "Il y avait en cette bande un Capitaine qui porte le nom le plus considerable de toute sa Nation, Sagochiendagehtè."--Relation of 1654, p. 8. Elsewhere, as in the Relation for 1657, p. 17, this name is spelt Agochiendagueté.

The name, it is said, was given to the nation because when Dekanawidah and Hiawatha first went to meet its chief, they crossed the Oneida creek on a bridge composed of an immense tree which had fallen or been laid across it, and noted that the Council fire at which the treaty was concluded was kindled against another huge log. These, however, may be merely explanations invented in later times.

The Cayugas bore in Council the name of Sotinonnawentona, meaning "the Great-Pipe People." In the singular it is Sononnawentona. The root of the word is kanonnawen, which in composition becomes kanonnawenta, meaning pipe, or calumet. It is said that the chief who in the first Council represented the Cayugas smoked a pipe of unusual size, which attracted the notice of the "name-givers."

Finally the Seneca mountaineers, the Sonnontowanas, bore the title, in the Canienga speech, of Ronaninhohonti, "the Door-keepers," or literally, "they who are at the doorway." In the singular this becomes Roninhohonti. In the Onondaga dialect it is Honinhohonta. It is a verbal form, derived from Kanhoha, door, and ont, to be. This name is undoubtedly coeval with the formation of the League, and was bestowed as a title of honor. The Senecas, at the western end of the "extended mansion," guarded the entrance against the wild tribes in that quarter, whose hostility was most to be dreaded.

The enumeration of the chiefs who formed the confederacy is closed by the significant words, "and then, in later times, additions were made to the great edifice." This is sufficient evidence that the Canienga "Book of Rites" was composed in its present form after the Tuscaroras, and possibly after the Nanticokes and Tuteloes, were received into the League. The Tuscaroras were admitted in 1714; the two other nations were received about the year 1753. [1]

An outburst of lamentation follows. The speaker has recited the names of the heroes and statesmen to whom the united nations were indebted for the Great Peace which had so long prevailed among them. He has recalled the wise laws which they established; and he is about to chant the closing litany, commemorating the fifty chiefs who composed the first federal

---

[1] The former date is well known; for the latter, see N. Y Hist. Col., Vol. 6, p. 311; Stone's Life of Sir William Johnson, p. 434.

council, and whose names have remained as the official titles of their successors. In recalling these memories of departed greatness his mind is filled with grief and humiliation at the contrast presented by the degeneracy of his own days. It is a common complaint of all countries and all times; but the sentiment was always, according to the missionaries, especially strong among the Indians, who are a conservative race. The orator appeals to the shades of their ancestors, in words which, in the baldest of literal versions, are full of eloquence and pathos. The "great law" has become old, and has lost its force. Its authors have passed away, and have carried it with them into their graves. They have placed it as a pillow under their heads. Their degenerate successors have inherited their names, but not their mighty intellects; and in the flourishing region which they left, nought but a desert remains. A trace, and not a slight one, of the mournful sublimity which we admire in the Hebrew prophets, with a similar cadence of "parallelism" in the style, will be noticed in this forest lament.

The same characteristics mark the chanted litany which closes the address. There is not merely parallelism and cadence, but occasionally rhyme, in the stanzas which are interspersed among the names, as is seen in the oft-repeated chorus which follows the names composing each clan or "class":--

> Etho natejonhne,
> Sewaterihwakhaonghkwe,
> Sewarihwisaanonghkwe,
> Kayanerenhkowa. [1]

This litany is sung in the usual style of their mourning or religious chants, with many long-drawn repetitions of the customary ejaculation haihhaih,-- an exclamation which, like the Greek "haí! haí!" belongs to the wailing style appropriate to such a monody. The expressions of the chant, like those of a Greek chorus, are abrupt, elliptical, and occasionally obscure. It is probable that this chant, like the condoling Hymn in the former part of the Book, is of earlier style than the other portions of the work, their rhythmical form having preserved the original wiords with greater accuracy. Such explanations of the doubtful passages as could be obtained from the chiefs and the interpreters will be found in the notes.

---

[1] For the translation, see ante, p. 33.

The chant and the Book end abruptly with the mournful exclamation, "Now we are dejected in mind." The lament which precedes the litany, and which is interrupted by it, may be said to close with these words. As the council is held, nominally at least, for the purpose of condolence, and as it necessarily revives the memory of the departed worthies of their republic, it is natural that the ceremonies throughout should be of a melancholy cast. They were doubtless so from the beginning, and before there was any occasion to deplore the decay of their commonwealth or the degeneracy of the age. In fact, when we consider that the founders of the League, with remarkable skill and judgment, managed to compress into a single day the protracted and wasteful obsequies customary among other tribes of the same race, we shall not be surprised to find that they sought to make the ceremonies of the day as solemn and impressive as possible.

But there are other characteristics of the "Book of Rites," prominent in the Canienga section, and still more marked in the Onondaga portion, which may well excite our astonishment. They have been already noticed, but seem to deserve fuller consideration. It will be observed that,.from beginning to end, the Book breathes nothing but sentiments of kindness and sympathy for the living, and of reverence for the departed,--not merely for the chief whom they have come to mourn, but also for the great men who have preceded him, and especially for the founders of their commonwealth. Combined with these sentiments, and harmonizing with them, is an earnest desire for peace, along with a profound respect for the laws under which they lived. The work in which these feelings are expressed is a genuine composition of the Indians themselves, framed long before they were affected by any influences from abroad, and repeated among them for centuries, with the entire assent of the hearers. It affords unquestionable evidence of the true character both of those who composed and of those who received it.

THE IROQUOIS CHARACTER

THE popular opinion of the Indian, and more especially of the Iroquois, who, as Mr. Parkman well observes, is an "Indian of the Indians," represents him as a sanguinary, treacherous and vindictive being, somewhat cold in his affections, haughty and reserved toward his friends, merciless to his enemies, fond of strife, and averse to industry and the pursuits of peace. Some magnanimous traits are occasionally allowed to him; and poetry and romance have sometimes thrown a glamour about his character, which popular opinion, not without reason, energeticaliy repudiates and resents. The truth is that the circumstances under which the red and white races have encountered in North America have been such as necessarily to give rise to a wholly false impression in regard to the character of the aborigines. The European colonists, superior in civilization and in the arts of war, landed on the coast with the deliberate intention of taking possession of the country and displacing the natives. The Indians were at once thrown on the defensive. From the very beginning they fought, not merely for their land, but for their lives; for it was from their land that they drew the means of living. All wars between the whites and the Indians, whatever the color or pretence on either side, have been on both sides wars of extermination. They have been carried on as such wars always have been and always will be carried on. On the side of the stronger there have been constant encroachments, effected now by menace and now by cajolery, but always prefaced by the display and the insolence of superior power. On the side of the weaker there have been alternations of sullen acquiescence and of fierce and fruitless resistance. It is not surprising that under such circumstances the character of each party has been presented to the other in the most forbidding light.

The Indians must be judged, like every other people, not by the traits which they display in the fury of a desperate warfare, but by their ordinary demeanor in time of peace, and especially by the character of their social and domestic life. On this point the testimony of missionaries and of other competent observers who have lived among them is uniform. At home the Indians are the most kindly and generous of men. Constant good humor, unfailing courtesy, ready sympathy with distress, and a truly lavish liberality, mark their intercourse with one another. The Jesuit missionaries among the Hurons knew them before intercourse with the whites and the use of ardent spirits had embittered and debased them. The testimony which they have left on record is very remarkable. The missionary Brebeuf, protesting against the ignorant prejudice which would place the Indians on a level with the brutes, gives the result of his observation in emphatic terms. "In my opinion," he writes, "it is no small matter to say of them that they live united in towns, sometimes of fifty, sixty, or a hundred dwellings, that is, of three or four hundred households; that they cultivate the fields, from which they derive their food for the whole year; and that they maintain peace and friendship with one another." He doubts "if there is another nation under heaven more commendable in this respect", than the Huron nation of the Bear," among whom he resided. "They have," he declares, "a gentleness and an affability almost incredible for barbarians." They keep up "this perfect goodwill," as he terms it, "by frequent visits, by the aid which they give one another in sickness, and. by their festivals and social gatherings, whenever they are not occupied by their fields and fisheries, or in hunting or trade." "They are," he continues, "less in their own cabins than in those of their friends. If any one falls sick, and wants something which may benefit him, everybody is eager to furnish it. Whenever one of them has something specially good to eat, he invites his friends and makes a feast. Indeed, they hardly ever eat alone." [1]

The Iroquois, who had seemed little better than demons to the missionaries while they knew them only as enemies to the French or their Huron allies, astonished them, on a nearer acquaintance, by the development of similar traits of natural goodness. "You will find in them," declares one of these fair-minded and cultivated observers, "virtues which might well put to blush the majority of Christians. There is no need of hospitals among them, because there are no beggars among them, and indeed, none who are poor, so long as any of them are rich. Their kindness, humanity and courtesy not merely make them liberal in giving, but almost lead them to live as though everything they possess were held in common. No one can want food while there is corn anywhere in the town." It is true that the missionaries often accuse the Iroquois of cruelty and perfidy; but the narrative shows that these qualities were only displayed in their wars, and apparently only against enemies whose cruelty and perfidy they had experienced.

---

[1] Relation for 1636, p. 117.

We can now see that the plan of universal federation and general peace which Hiawatha devised had nothing in itself so surprising as to excite our incredulity. It was, indeed, entirely in accordance with the genius of his people. Its essence was the extension to all nations of the methods of social and civil life which prevailed in his own nation. If the people of a town of four hundred families could live in constant "peace and friendship," why should not all the tribes of men dwell together in the same manner? The idea is one which might readily have occurred to any man of benevolent feelings and thoughtful temperament. The project in itself is not so remarkable as the energy and skill with which it was carried into effect. It is deserving of notice, however, that according to the Indian tradition, Hiawatha was impelled to action mainly by experience of the mischiefs which were caused in his own nation through a departure from their ordinary system of social life. The missionaries, in describing the general harmony which prevailed among the Hurons, admit that it was sometimes disturbed. There were "bad spirits" among them, as everywhere else, who could not always be controlled.[1] Atotarho, among the Onondagas, was one of these bad spirits; and in his case, unfortunately, an evil disposition was reinforced by a keen intellect and a powerful will. His history for a time offered a rare instance of something approaching to despotism, or the Greek "tyranny," exercised in an Indian tribe. A fact so strange, and conduct so extraordinary, seemed in aftertimes to require explanation. A legend is preserved among the Onondagas, which was apparently devised to account for a prodigy so far out of the common order of events. I give it in the words in which it is recorded in my journal.[2]

"Another legend, of which I have not before heard, professed to give the origin both of the abnormal ferocity and of the preterhuman powers of Atotarho. He was already noted as a chief and a warrior, when he had the misfortune to kill a peculiar bird, resembling a sea-gull, which is reputed to possess poisonous qualities of singular virulence. By his contact with the dead bird his mind was affected. He became morose and cruel, and at the same time obtained the power of destroying men and other creatures at a distance. Three sons of Hiawatha were among his victims. He attended the

---

[1] Relation of 1636, p. 118: "Ostez quelques mauvais esprits, qui se rencontrent quasi partout," etc.
[2] This story was related to me in March, 1882, by my intelligent friend, Chief John Buck, who was inclined to give it credence,--sharing in this, as in other things, the sentiments of the best among his people.

Councils which were held, and made confusion in them, and brought all the people into disturbance and terror. His bodily appearance was changed at the same time, and his aspect became so terrible that the story spread, and was believed, that his head was encircled by living snakes."

The only importance of this story is in the evidence it affords that conduct so anti-social as that of Atotarho was deemed to be the result of a disordered mind. In his case, as in that of the Scottish tyrant and murderer, "the insane root that took the reason prisoner," was doubtless an unbridled ambition. It is interesting to remark that even his fierce temper and determined will were forced to yield at last to the pressure of public opinion, which compelled him to range himself on the side of peace and union. In the whimsical imagery of the narrative, which some of the story-tellers, after their usual fashion, have converted from a metaphor to a fact, Hiawatha "combed the snakes out of the head" of his great antagonist, and presented him to the Council changed and restored to his right mind.

THE IROQUOIS POLICY

FEW popular notions, it may be affirmed, are so far from the truth as that which makes the Iroquois a band of treacherous and ferocious ravagers, whose career was marked everywhere by cruelty and devastation. The clear and positive evidence of historical facts leads to a widely different conclusion. It is not going too far to assert that among all uncivilized races the Iroquois have shown themselves to be the most faithful of allies, the most placable of enemies, and the most clement of conquerors. It will be proper, in justice to them, as well as in the interest of political and social science, to present briefly the principles and methods which guided them in their intercourse with other communities. Their system, as finally developed, comprised four distinct forms of connection with other nations, all tending directly to the establishment of universal peace.

1. As has been already said, the primary object of the founders of their League was the creation of a confederacy which should comprise all the nations and tribes of men that were known to them. Experience, however, quickly showed that this project, admirable in idea, was impossible of execution. Distance, differences of language, and difficulties of communication, presented obstacles which could not be overcome. But the plan was kept in view as one of the cardinal principles of their policy. They were always eager to receive new members into their League. The Tuscaroras, the Nanticokes, the Tuteloes, and a band of the Delawares, were thus successively admitted, and all of them still retain representatives in the Council of the Canadian branch of the confederacy.

2. When this complete political union could not be achieved, the Iroquois sought to accomplish the same end, as far as possible, by a treaty of alliance. Two notable examples will show how earnestly this purpose was pursued, and how firmly it was maintained. When the Dutch established their trading settlements on the Hudson River, one of their first proceedings was to send an embassy to the Five Nations, with proposals for a treaty. The overture was promptly accepted. A strict alliance was formed, and was ratified in the usual manner by an exchange of wampum belts. When the English took the place of the Dutch, the treaty was renewed with

them, and was confirmed in the same manner. The wampum-belts then received by the Confederates are still preserved on their Canadian Reservation, and are still brought forth and expounded by the older chiefs to the younger generation, in their great Councils. History records with what unbroken faith, through many changes, and despite many provocations from their allies and many enticements from the French rulers and missionaries, this alliance was maintained to the last.

If it be suggested that this fidelity was strengthened by motives of policy, the same cannot be affirmed of the alliance with the Ojibways, which dates from a still earlier period. The annalists of the Kanonsionni affirm that their first treaty with this wide-spread people of the northwest was made soon after the formation of their League, and that it was strictly maintained on both sides for more than two hundred years. The Ojibways then occupied both shores of Lake Superior, and the northern part of the peninsula of Michigan. The point at which they came chiefly in contact with the adventurous Iroquois voyagers was at the great fishing station of St. Mary's Falls, on the strait which unites Lake Superior with Lake Huron,; and here, it is believed, the first alliance was consummated. After more than two centuries had elapsed, the broken bands of the defeated Hurons, fleeing from their ravaged homes on the Georgian Bay, took refuge among the Ojibways, with whom they, too, had always maintained a friendly understanding. Their presence and the story of their sufferings naturally awakened the sympathy of their hosts. The rapid spread of the Iroquois empire created alarm. A great agitation ensued among the far-dispersed bands of the Ojibway name. Occasional meetings between hunting-parties of the younger warriors of the two peoples,--the Iroquois arrogant in the consciousness of their recent conquests, the Ojibways sullen and suspicious,--led to bitter words, and sometimes to actual strife. On two occasions several Ojibway warriors were slain, under what provocation is uncertain. But the reparation demanded by the Ojibway chiefs was promptly conceded by the Iroquois Council. The amplest apology was made, and for every slain warrior a pack of furs was delivered. The ancient treaty was at the same time renewed, with every formality. Nothing could more clearly show the anxiety of the Iroquois rulers to maintain their national faith than this apology and reparation, so readily made by them, at the time when their people were at the height of their power and in the full flush of conquest.[1] These efforts, however, to preserve the ancient amity proved unavailing. Through whose fault it was that the final outbreak occurred is a question on which the annalists of the two parties differ. But the events just recounted, and, indeed, all the circumstances, speak strongly in favor of the Iroquois. They had shown their anxiety to maintain the peace, and they had nothing to gain by war. The bleak northern home of the Ojibways offered no temptation to the most greedy conqueror. To the Ojibways, on the other hand, the broad expanse of western Canada, now lying deserted, and stretching before them its wealth of forests full of deer, its lakes and rivers swarming with fish, its lovely glades and fertile plains, where the corn harvests of the Hurons and Neutrals had lately glistened, were an allurement which they could not resist. They assumed at once the wrongs and the territories of their exiled Huron friends, and plunged into the long-meditated strife with their ancient allies. The contest was desperate and destructive. Many sanguinary battles took place, and great numbers of warriors fell on both sides. On the whole the balance inclined against the Iroquois. In this war they were a southern people, contending against a hardier race from the far north. They fought at a distance from their homes, while the Ojibways, migrating in bands, pitched their habitations in the disputed region.

Finally, both sides became weary of the strife. Old sentiments of fellowship revived. Peace was declared, and a new treaty was made. The territory for which they had fought was divided between them. The southwestern portion, which had been the home of the Attiwandaronks, remained as the hunting-ground of the Iroquois. North and east of this section the Ojibways possessed the land. The new treaty, confirmed by the exchange of wampum-belts and by a peculiar interlocking of the right arms, which has ever since been the special sign of amity between the Iroquois and the Ojibways, was understood to make them not merely allies but brothers. As the symbol on one of the belts which is still preserved indicates, they were to be as relatives who are so nearly akin that they eat from the same dish. This treaty, made two centuries ago, has ever since been religiously maintained. Its effects are felt to this day. Less than forty years ago a band

---

[1] The Ojibway historian, Copway, in his "Traditional History of the Ojibway Nation" (p. 84), gives the particulars of this event, as preserved by the Ojibways themselves. Even the strong national prejudice of the narrator, which has evidently colored his statement, leaves the evidence of the magnanimity and prudence of the Iroquois elders clearly apparent.

The Iroquois Book of Rites

of the Ojibways, the Missisagas, forced to relinquish their reserved lands on the River Credit, sought a refuge with the Iroquois of the Grand River Reservation. They appealed to this treaty, and to the evidence of the wampum-belts. Their appeal was effectual. A large tract of valuable land was granted to them by the Six Nations. Here, maintaining their distinct tribal organization, they still reside, a living evidence of the constancy and liberality with which the Iroquois uphold their treaty obligations.

3. When a neighboring people would neither join the confederacy nor enter into a treaty of alliance with it, the almost inevitable result would be, sooner or later, a deadly war. Among the nomadic or unsettled Indian tribes, especially the Algonkins and Sioux, the young men are expected to display their bravery by taking scalps; and a race of farmers, hunters, and fishermen, like the Iroquois, would be tempting victims. Before the confederacy was formed, some of its members, particularly the Caniengas and Oneidas, had suffered greatly from wars with the wilder tribes about them. The new strength derived from the League enabled them to turn the tables upon their adversaries. But they made a magnanimous use of their superiority. An enemy who submitted was at once spared. When the great Delaware nation, the Lenapes, known as the head of the Algonkin stock, yielded to the arms of the Kanonsionni, they were allowed to retain their territory and nearly all their property. They were simply required to acknowledge themselves the subjects of the Iroquois, to pay a moderate tribute in wampum and furs, and to refrain thenceforth from taking any part in war. In the expressive Indian phrase, they were "made women." This phrase did not even imply, according to Iroquois ideas, any serious humiliation; for among them, as the French missionaries tell us, women had much authority. [1] Their special office in war was that of peace-makers. It was deemed to be their right and duty, when in their opinion the strife had lasted long enough, to interfere and bring about a reconciliation. The knowledge of this fact led the Lenapes, in aftertimes, to put forward a whimsical claim to dignity, which was accepted by their worthy but credulous historian, Heckewelder. They asserted that while their nation was at the height of power, their ancestors were persuaded by the insidious wiles of the Iroquois to lay aside their arms, for the purpose of assuming the lofty position of universal mediators and arbiters among the

---

[1] "Les femmes ayant beaucoup d'autorité parmi ces peuples, leur vertu y fait d'autant plus de fruit qu'autre part."--Relation of 1657, p. 48.

Indian nations.[1] That this preposterous story should have found credence is surprising enough. A single fact suffices to disprove it, and to show the terms on which the Delawares stood with the great northern confederacy. Colden has preserved for us the official record of the Council which was held in Philadelphia, in July, 1742, between the provincial authorities and the deputies of the Six Nations, headed by their noted orator and statesman, the great Onondaga chief, Canasatego. The Delawares, whose claim to certain lands was to be decided, attended the conference. The Onondaga leader, after reciting the evidence which had been laid before him to show that these lands had been sold to the colonists by the Delawares, and severely rebuking the latter for their breach of faith in repudiating the bargain, continued: "But how came you to take upon you to sell land at all? We conquered you. We made women of you. You know you are women, and can no more sell land than women. Nor is it fit that you should have the power of selling lands, since you would abuse it. This very land that you now claim has been consumed by you. You have had it in meat and drink and clothes, and now you want it again, like children, as you are. But what makes you sell land in the dark? Did you ever tell us that you had sold this land? Did we ever receive any part of the price, even the value of a pipe-stem from you? You have told us a blind story--that you sent a messenger to inform us of the sale; but he never came among us, nor have we ever heard anything about it. And for all these reasons we charge you to remove instantly. We don't give you the liberty to think about it. We assign you two places to go, either to Wyoming or Shamokin. You may go to either of those places, and then we shall have you more under our eyes, and shall see how you behave. Don't deliberate, but remove away; and take this belt of wampum." [2]

This imperious allocution, such as a Cinna or a Cornelius might have delivered to a crowd of trembling and sullen Greeks, shows plainly enough the relation in which the two communities stood to one another. It proves also that the rule under which the conquered Delawares were held was anything but oppressive. They seem to have been allowed almost entire freedom, except only in making war and in disposing of their lands without the consent of the Six Nations. In fact, the Iroquois, in dealing with them, anticipated the very regulations which the enlightened governments of the United States and England now enforce in that benevolent treatment of

---

[1] Heckewelder's History of the Indian Nations, p. 56.
[2] Colden: History of the Five Nations, Vol. II, p. 36 (2d Edition).

the Indian tribes for which they justly claim high credit. Can they refuse a like credit to their dusky predecessors and exemplars, or deny them the praise of being, as has been already said, the most clement of conquerors?

4. Finally, when a tribe within what may be called "striking distance" of the Confederacy would neither join the League, nor enter into an alliance with its members, nor come under their protection, there remained nothing but a chronic state of warfare, which destroyed all sense of security and comfort. The Iroquois hunter, fisherman, or trader, returning home after a brief absence, could never be sure that he would not find his dwelling a heap of embers, smouldering over the mangled remains of his wife and children. The plainest dictates of policy taught the Confederates that the only safe method in dealing with such persistent and unappeasable foes was to crush them utterly. Among the most dangerous of their enemies were the Hurons and the eastern Algonkins, sustained and encouraged by the French colonists. It is from them and their historians chiefly that the complaints of Iroquois cruelties have descended to us; but the same historians have not omitted to inform us that the first acquaintance of the Iroquois with these colonists was through two most wanton and butcherly assaults which Champlain and his soldiers, in company with their Indian allies, made upon their unoffending neighbors. No milder epithets can justly describe these unprovoked invasions, in which the Iroquois bowmen, defending their homes, were shot down mercilessly with firearms, by strangers whom they had never before seen or perhaps even heard of. This stroke of evil policy, which tarnished an illustrious name, left far-reaching consequences, affecting the future of half a continent. Its first result was the destruction of the Hurons, the special allies and instigators of the colonists in their hostilities. The Attiwandaronks, or Neutrals, with whom, till this time, the Iroquois had maintained peaceful relations, shared the same fate; for they were the friends of the Hurons and the French. The Eries perished in a war provoked, as the French missionaries in their always trustworthy accounts inform us, by a perverse freak of cruelty on their own part.

Yet, in all these destructive wars, the Iroquois never for a moment forgot the principles which lay at the foundation of their League, and which taught them to "strengthen their house" by converting enemies into friends. On the instant that resistance ceased, slaughter ceased with it. The warriors who were willing to unite their fortunes with the Confederates were at once welcomed among them. Some were adopted into the families of those who had lost children or brothers. Others had lands allotted to them, on which they were allowed to live by themselves, under their own chiefs and their native laws, until in two or three generations, by friendly intercourse, frequent intermarriages, and community of interests, they became gradually absorbed into the society about them. Those who suppose that the Hurons only survive in a few Wyandots, and that the Eries, Attiwandaronks, and Andastes have utterly perished, are greatly mistaken. It is absolutely certain that of the twelve thousand Indians who now, in the United States and Canada, preserve the Iroquois name, the greater portion derive their descent, in whole or in part, from those conquered nations.[1] No other Indian. community, so far as we know' has ever pursued this policy of incorporation to anything near the same extent, or carried it out with anything like the same humanity. Even towards the most determined and the most savage of their foes, the Kanonsionni, when finally victorious, showed themselves ever magnanimous and placable.

The common opinion of the cruelty of the Iroquois has arisen mainly from the custom which they occasionally practiced, like some other Indians, of burning prisoners at the stake. Out of the multitude of their captives, the

---

[1] Ces victoires leur causant presque autant de perte qu'à leurs ennemis, elles ont tellement depeuplé leurs Bourgs, qu'on y compte plus d'Estrangers que de naturels du pays. Onnontaghé a sept nations differentes qui s'y sont venües establir, et il s'en trouve jusqu'à onze dans Sonnontoüan." Relation of 1657, p. 34, "Qui feroit la supputation des francs Iroquois, auroit de la peine d'en trouver plus de douze cents (i.e. combattans) en toutes les cinq Nations, parce que le plus grand nombre n'est composé que d'un ramas de divers peuples qu'ils ont conquestez, commes des Hurons, des Tionnontateronnons, autrement Nation du Petun; des Attiwendaronk, qu'on appelloit Neutres, quand ils estoient sur pied; des Riquehronnons, qui sont ceux de la Nation des Chats; des Ont8aganha, ou Nation du Feu; des Trak8aehronnons, et autres, qui, tout estrangers qu'ils sont, font sans doute la plus grande et la meilleure parties des Iroquois." Rel. de 1660, p. 7. Yet, it was this "conglomeration of divers peuples" that, under the discipline of Iroquois institutions and the guidance of Iroquois statesmen and commanders, held high the name of the Kanonsionni, and made the Confederacy a great power on the continent for more than a century after this time; who again and again measured arms and intellects with French generals and diplomatists, and came off at least with equal fortune; who smote their Abenaki enemies in the far east, punished the Illinois marauders in the far west, and thrust back the intruding Cherokees into their southern mountains; who were a wall of defence to the English colonies, and a strong protection to the many broken bands of Indians which from every quarter clustered round the shadow of the "great pine tree" of Onondaga.

The Iroquois Book of Rites

number subjected to this torture was really very small,--probably not nearly as large in proportion as the number of criminals and political prisoners who, in some countries of Europe, at about the same time, were subjected to the equally cruel torments of the rack and the wheel. These criminals and other prisoners were so tortured because they were regarded as the enemies of society. The motives which actuated the Iroquois were precisely the same. As has been before remarked, the mode in which their enemies carried on their warfare with them was chiefly by stealthy and sudden inroads. The prowling warrior lurked in the woods near the Iroquois village through the day, and at night fell with hatchet and club upon his unsuspecting victims. The Iroquois lawgivers deemed it essential for the safety of their people that the men who were guilty of such murderous attacks should have reason to apprehend, if caught, a direful fate.

If the comparatively few instances of these political tortures which occurred among the Iroquois are compared with the awful list of similar and worse inflictions which stain the annals of the most enlightened nations of Europe and Asia, ancient and modern,--the crucifixions, the impalements, the dreadful mutilations--lopping of hands and feet, tearing out of eyes--the tortures of the rack and wheel, the red-hot pincers, the burning crown, the noisome dungeon, the slow starvation, the lingering death in the Siberian mines,--it will become evident that these barbarians were far inferior to their civilized contemporaries in the temper and arts of inhumanity. Even in the very method of punishment which they adopted the Indians were outdone in Europe, and that, strangely enough, by the two great colonizing and conquering nations, heirs of all modern enlightenment, who came to displace them,--the English and the Spaniards. The Iroquois never burnt women at the stake. To put either men or women to death for a difference of creed had not occurred to them. It may justly be affirmed that in the horrors of Smithfield and the Campo Santo, the innate barbarism of the Aryan, breaking through his thin varnish of civilization, was found far transcending the utmost barbarism of the Indian. [1]

---

[1] The Aryans of Europe are undoubtedly superior in humanity, courage and independence, to those of Asia. It is possible that the finer qualities which distinguish the western branch of this stock may have been derived from admixture with an earlier population of Europe, identical in race and character with the aborigines of America. See Appendix, Note F.

THE IROQUOIS LANGUAGE

AS the mental faculties of a people are reflected in their speech, we should naturally expect that the language of a race manifesting such unusual powers as the Iroquois nations have displayed would be of a remarkable character. In this expectation we are not disappointed. The languages of the Huron-Iroquois family belong to what has been termed the polysynthetic class, and are distinguished, even in that class, by a more than ordinary endowment of that variety of forms and fullness of expression for which languages of that type are noted. The best-qualified judges have been the most struck with this peculiar excellence. "The variety of compounds," wrote the accomplished missionary, Brebeuf, concerning the Huron tongue, "is very great; it is the key to the secret of their language. They have as many genders as ourselves, as many numbers as the Greeks." Recurring to the same comparison, he remarks of the Huron verb that it has as many tenses and numbers as the Greek, with certain discriminations which the latter did not possess. [1] A great living authority has added the weight of his name to these opinions of the scholarly Jesuit. Professor Max Müller, who took the opportunity afforded by the presence of a Mohawk undergraduate at Oxford to study his language, writes of it in emphatic terms: "To my mind the structure of such a language as the Mohawk is quite sufficient evidence that those who worked out such a work of art were powerful reasoners; and accurate classifiers." [2]

---

[1] Relation of 1636, pp. 99, 100.

[2] in a letter to the author, dated Feb. 14, 1882. in a subsequent letter Prof. Müller writes, in regard to the study of the aboriginal languages of this continent: "It has long been a puzzle to me why this most tempting p. 100 and promising field of philological research has been allowed to lie almost fallow in America,--as if these languages could not tell us quite as much of the growth of the human mind as Chinese, or Hebrew, or Sanscrit." I have Prof. Max Müller's permission to publish these extracts, and gladly do so, in the hope that they may serve to stimulate that growing interest which the efforts of scholars like Trumbull, Shea, Cuoq, Brinton, and, more recently, Major Powell and his able collaborators of the Ethnological Bureau, are at length beginning to awaken among us, in the investigation of this important and almost unexplored province of linguistic science.

The Iroquois Book of Rites

It is a fact somewhat surprising, as well as unfortunate, that no complete grammar of any language of the Huron-Iroquois stock has ever been published. Many learned and zealous missionaries, Catholic and Protestant, have labored among the tribes of this stock for more than two centuries. Portions of the Scriptures, as well as some other works, have been translated into several of these languages. Some small books, including biographies and hymn-books, have been composed and printed in two of them; and the late devoted and indefatigable missionary among the Senecas, the Rev. Asher Wright, conducted for several years a periodical, the "Mental Elevator" (Ne Jaguhnigoageswatha), in their language. Several grammars are known to have been composed, but none have as yet been printed in a complete form. One reason of this unwillingness to publish was, undoubtedly, the sense which the compilers felt of the insufficiency of their work. Such is the extraordinary complexity of the language, such the multiplicity of its forms and the subtlety of its distinctions, that years of study are required to master it; and indeed it may be said that the abler the investigator and the more careful his study, the more likely he is to be dissatisfied with his success. This dissatisfaction was frankly expressed and practically exhibited by Mr. Wright himself, certainly one of the best endowed and most industrious of these inquirers. After residing for several years among the Senecas, forming an alphabet remarkable for its precise discrimination of sounds, and even publishing several translations in their language, he undertook to give some account of its grammatical forms. A little work printed in 1842, with the modest title of "A Spelling-book of the Seneca Language," comprises the variations of nouns, adjectives and pronouns, given with much minuteness. Those of the verbs are promised, but the book closes abruptly without them, for the reason--as the author afterwards explained to a correspondent--that he had not as yet been able to obtain such a complete knowledge of them as he desired. This difficulty is further exemplified by a work purporting to be a "Grammar of the Huron Language, by a Missionary of the Village of Huron Indians near Quebec, found amongst the papers of the Mission, and translated from the Latin, by the Rev. John Wilkie." This translation is published in the "Transactions of the Literary and Historical Society of Quebec," for 1831, and fills more than a hundred octavo pages. It is a work evidently of great labor, and is devoted chiefly to the variations of the verbs; yet its lack of completeness may be judged from the single fact that the "transitions," or in other words, the combinations of the double pronouns, nominative and objective, with the transitive verb, which form such an important feature of the language, are hardly noticed; and, it may be added, though the conjugations are mentioned, they are not explained. The work, indeed, would rather perplex than aid an investigator, and gives no proper idea of the character and richness of the language. The same may be said of the grammatical notices comprised in the Latin "Proemium" to Bruyas' Iroquois dictionary. These notices are apparently modeled to some extent on this anonymous grammar of the Huron language,--unless, indeed, the latter may have been copied from Bruyas; the rules which they give being in several instances couched in the same words.

Some useful grammatical explanations are found in the anonymous Onondaga dictionary of the seventeenth century, published by Dr. Shea in his "Library of American linguistics." But by far the most valuable contribution to our knowledge of the structure of this remarkable group of languages is found in the works of a distinguished writer of our own day, the Rev. J. A. Cuoq, of Montreal, eminent both as a missionary and as a philologist. After twenty years of labor among the Iroquois and Algonkin tribes in the Province of Quebec, M. Cuoq was led to appear as an author by his desire to defend his charges against the injurious effect of a judgment which had been pronounced by a noted authority. M. Renan had put forth, among the many theories which distinguish his celebrated work on the Semitic languages, one which seemed to M. Cuoq as mischievous as it was unfounded. M. Renan held that no races were capable of civilization except such as have now attained it; and that these comprised only the Aryan, the Semitic, and the Chinese. This opinion was enforced by a reference to the languages spoken by the members of those races. "To imagine a barbarous race speaking a Semitic or an Indo-European language is," he declares, "an impossible supposition (une fiction contradiaoire), which no person can entertain who is familiar with the laws of comparative philology, and with the general theory of the human intellect." To one who remembers that every nation of the Indo-European race traces its descent from a barbarous ancestry, and especially that the Germans in the days of Tacitus were in precisely the same social stage as that of the Iroquois in the days of Champlain, this opinion of the brilliant French philologist and historian will seem erratic and unaccountable. M. Cuoq sought to refute it, not merely by argument, but by the logic of facts. In two works, published successively in 1864 and 1866, he showed, by many and various examples, that the Iroquois and Algonkin languages possessed all the excellences which M. Renan admired in the Indo-European languages, and surpassed in

The Iroquois Book of Rites

almost every respect the Semitic and Chinese tongues. [1] The resemblances of these Indian languages to the Greek struck him, as it had struck his illustrious predecessor, the martyred Brebeuf, two hundred years before. M. Cuoq is also the author of a valuable Iroquois lexicon, with notes and appendices, in which he discusses some interesting points in the philology of the language. This lexicon is important, also, for comparison with that of the Jesuit missionary, Bruyas, as showing how little the language has varied in the course of two centuries. [2] The following particulars respecting the Iroquois tongues are mainly derived from the works of M. Cuoq, of Bruyas, and of Mr. Wright, supplemented by the researches of the author, pursued at intervals during several years, among the tribes of Western Canada and New York. Only a very brief sketch of the subject can here be given. It is not too much to say that a complete grammar of any Iroquois language would be at least as extensive as the best Greek or Sanscrit grammar. For such a work neither the writer, nor perhaps any other person now living, except M. Cuoq himself, would be competent.

The phonology of the language is at once simple and perplexing. According to M. Cuoq, twelve letters suffice to represent it: a, e, f, h, i, k, n, o, r, s, t, w. Mr. Wright employs for the Seneca seventeen, with diacritical marks, which raise the number to twenty-one. The English missionaries among the Mohawks found sixteen letters sufficient, a, d, e, g, h, i, j, k, n, o, r, s, t, u, w, y. There are no labial sounds, unless the f, which rarely occurs, and appears to be merely an aspirated w, may be considered one. No definite distinction is maintained between the vowel sounds o and u, and one of these letters may be dispensed with. The distinction between hard and soft (or surd and sonant) mutes is not preserved. The sounds of d and t, and those of k and g, are interchangeable. So also are those of l and r, the former sound being heard more frequently in the Oneida dialect and the latter in the Canienga. From the Western dialects,--the Onondaga, Cayuga and

---

[1] See Jugement Erroné de M. Ernest Renan sur les Langues Sauvages: (2d edit.) Dawson Brothers, Montreal: 1870; and Études Philologiques sur quelques Langues Sauvages de l'Amérique. Par N. O., Ancien Missionaire. Ibid: 1866. Also Lexique de la Langue Iroquoise, avec notes et appendices. Par J. A. Cuoq, Prêtre de St. Sulpice. J. Chapleau & Fils, Montreal: 1882. These are all works indispensable to the student of Indian languages.

[2] Radices Verborum Iroquæorum. Auctore R. p. Jacopo Bruyas, Societatis Jesu. Published in Shea's "Library of American Linguistics." For the works in this invaluable Library, American scholars owe a debt of gratitude to Dr. Shea's enlightened zeal in the cause of science and humanity.

Seneca,--this l or r sound has, in modern times, disappeared altogether. The Canienga konoronkwa, I esteem him (in Oneida usually sounded konolonkwa), has become konoenkwa in Onondaga, and in Cayuga and Seneca is contracted to kononkwa. Aspirates and aspirated gutturals abound, and have been variously represented by h, hh, kh, and gh, and sometimes (in the works of the early French missionaries) by the Greek chi and the spiritus asper. Yet no permanent distinction appears to be maintained among the sounds thus represented, and M. Cuoq reduces them all to the simple h. The French nasal sound abounds. M. Cuoq and the earlier English missionaries have expressed it, as in French, simply by the n when terminating a syllable. When it does not close a syllable, a diæresis above the n, or else the Spanish tilde (ñ) indicates the sound. Mr. Wright denotes it by a line under the vowel. The later English missionaries express it by a diphthong: ken becomes kea; nonwa becomes noewa; onghwentsya is written oughweatsya.

A strict analysis would probably reduce the sounds of the Canienga language to seven consonants, h, k, n. r, s, t, and w, and four vowels, a, e, i, and o, of which three, a, e, and o, may receive a nasal sound. This nasalizing makes them, in fact, distinct elements; and the primary sounds of the language may therefore be reckoned at fourteen. [1] The absence of labials and the frequent aspirated gutturals give to the utterance of the best speakers a deep and sonorous character which reminds the hearer of the stately Castilian speech.

The "Book of Rites," or, rather, the Canienga portion of it, is written in the orthography first employed by the English missionaries. The d is frequently used, and must be regarded merely as a variant of the t sound. The g is sometimes, though rarely, employed as a variant of the k. The digraph gh is common and represents the guttural aspirate, which in German is indicated by ch and in Spanish by j. The French missionaries write it now simply h, and consider it merely a harsh pronunciation of the aspirate. The j is sounded as in English; it usually represents a complex sound, which might be analysed into ts or tsï; jathondek is properly tsïatontek. The x, which occasionally appears, is to be pronounced ks, as in English. An, en, on,

---

[1] A dental t,--which the French missionaries represent sometimes by the Greek theta and sometimes by th, and which the English have also occasionally expressed by the latter method, may possibly furnish an additional element. The Greek 8 of the former is simply the English w.

The Iroquois Book of Rites

when not followed by a vowel, have a nasal sound, as in French. This sound is heard even when those syllables are followed by another n. Thus Kanonsionni is pronounced as if written Kanoñsioñni and yondennase as if written yoñdeñnase. The vowels have usually the same sound as in German and Italian; but in the nasal en the vowel has an obscure sound, nearly like that of the short u in but. Thus yondennase sounds almost as if written yoñduñnase, and kanienke is pronounced nearly like kaniuñke.

The nouns in Iroquois are varied, but with accidence differing from the Aryan and Semitic variations, some of the distinctions being more subtle, and, so to speak, metaphysical. The dual is expressed by prefixing the particle te, and suffixing ke to the noun; thus., from kanonsa, house, we have tekanonsake, two houses. These syllables, or at least the first, are supposed to be derived from tekeni, two. The plural, when it follows an adjective expressive of number, is indicated by the syllable ni prefixed to the noun, and ke suffixed; as, eso nikanonsake, many houses. In other cases the plural is sometimes expressed by one of the words okon (or hokon) okonha, son and sonha, following the noun. In general, however, the plural significance of nouns is left to be inferred from the context, the verb always and the adjective frequently indicating it.

All beings are divided into two classes, which do not correspond either with the Aryan genders or with the distinctions of animate and inanimate which prevail in the Algonkin tongues. These classes have been styled noble and common. To the noble belong male human beings and deities. The other class comprises women and all other objects. It seems probable, however, that the distinction in the first instance was merely that of sex,--that it was, in fact, a true gender. Deities, being regarded as male, were included in the masculine gender. There being no neuter form, the feminine gender was extended, and made to comprise all other beings. These classes, however, are not indicated by any change in the noun, but merely by the forms of the pronoun and the verb.

The local relations of nouns are expressed by affixed particles, such as ke, ne, kon, akon, akta. Thus, from onónta mountain, we have onontáke, at (or to) the mountain; from akérat, dish, akehrátne, in (or on) the dish; from kanónsa, house, kanonsákon, or kanónskon, in the house, kanonsákon, under the house, and kanonsákta, near the house. These locative particles, it will be seen, usually, though not always, draw the accent towards them.

The most peculiar and perplexing variation is that made by what is termed the "crement," affixed to many (though not all) nouns. This crement in the Canienga takes various forms, ta, sera, tsera, kwa. Onkwe, man, becomes onkwéta; otkon, spirit, otkónsera; akáwe, oar, akawétsera; ahta, shoe, ahhtákwa. The crement is employed when the noun is used with numeral adjectives, when it has adjective or other affixes, and generally when it enters into composition with other words. Thus onkwe, man, combined with the adjective termination iyo (from the obsolete wiyo, good) becomes onkwetiyo, good man. Wenni, day, becomes in the plural niate niwennise-rake, many days, etc. The change, however, is not grammatical merely, but conveys a peculiar shade of meaning difficult to define. The noun, according to M. Cuoq, passes from a general and determinate to a special and restricted sense. Onkwe means man in general; asen nionkwetake, three men (in particular.) One interpreter rendered akawétsera, "the oar itself." The affix sera or tsera seems to be employed to form what we should term abstract nouns, though to the Iroquois mind they apparently present themselves as possessing a restricted or specialized sense. Thus from iotarihen, it is warm, we have otarihénsera, heat; from wakeriat, to be brave, ateriatítsera, courage. So kakweniátsera, authority; kanaiésera, pride; kanakwénsera, anger. Words of this class abound in the Iroquois; so little ground is there for the common opinion that the language is destitute of abstract nouns. [1]

The adjective, when employed in an isolated form, follows the substantive; as kanonsa kowa, large house; onkwe honwe (or onwe) a real man. But, in general, the substantive and the adjective coalesce in one word. Ase signifies new, and added to kanonsa gives us kanonsáse, new house. Karonta, tree, and kowa, or kowanen, great, make together karontowánen, great tree. Frequently the affixed adjective is never employed as an isolated word, The termination iyo (or iio) expresses good or beautiful, and aksen, bad or ugly; thus kanonsíyo, fine house, kanonsáksen, ugly house. These compound forms frequently make their plural by adding s, as kanonsíyos, kanonaksens.

The pronouns are more numerous than in any European language, and show clearer distinctions in meaning. Thus, in the singular, besides the

---

[1] See, on this point, the remarks of Dr. Brinton to the same effect, in regard to the Aztec, Qquichua, and other languages, with interesting illustrations, in his "American Hero Myths," p. 25

ordinary pronouns, I, thou, he and she, the language possesses an indeterminate form, which answers very nearly to the French on. The first person of the dual has two forms, the one including, the other excluding, the person addressed, and signifying, therefore, respectively,--"thou and I," and "he and I." The first person plural has the same twofold form. The third persons dual and plural have masculine and feminine forms. Thus the language has fifteen personal pronouns, all in common use, and all, it may be added, useful in expressing distinctions which the English can only indicate by circumlocutions. These pronouns are best shown in the form in which they are prefixed to a verb. The following are examples of the verb katkahtos, I see (root atkahto) and kenonwes, I love (root nonwe), as conjugated in the present tense:--

katkahtos, I see.
satkahtos, thou seest.
ratkahtos, he sees.
watkahtos, she sees.
iontkahtos, one sees.
tiatkahtos, we two see (thou and I.)
iakiatkahtos, we two see (he and I.)
tsiatkahtos, ye two see.
hiatkahtos, they two see (masc.)
kiatkahtos, they two see (fem.)
tewatkahtos, we see (ye and I.)
iakwatkahtos, we see (they and I.)
sewatkahtos, ye see.
rontkahtos, they see (masc.)
kontkahtos, they see (fem.)

kenonwes, I love.
senonwes, thou lovest.
rononwes, he loves.
kanonwes, she loves.
ienonwes, one loves.
teninonwes, we two love (thou and I)
iakeninonwes, we two love (he and I)
seninonwes, ye two love.
hninonwes, they two love (masc.)
keninonwes, they two love (fem.)
tewanonwes, we love (ye and I.)
iakwanonwes, we love (they and I.)
sewanonwes, ye love.
ratinonwes, they love (masc.)
kontinonwes, they love (fem.)

It will be observed that in these examples the prefixed pronouns differ considerably in some cases. These differences determine (or are determined by) the conjugation of the verbs. Katkahtos belongs to the first conjugation, and kenonwes to the second. There are three other conjugations, each of which shows some peculiarity in the prefixed pronouns, though, in the main, a general resemblance runs through them all. There are other variations of the pronouns, according to the "paradigm," as it is called, to which the verb belongs. Of these paradigms there are two, named in the modern Iroquois grammars paradigms K and A, from the first or characteristic letter of the first personal pronoun. The particular conjugation and paradigm to which any verb belongs can only be learned by practice, or from the dictionaries.

The same prefixed pronouns are used, with some slight variations, as possessives, when prefixed to a substantive; as, from sita, foot, we have (in Paradigm A) akasita, my foot, sasita, thy foot, raosita, his foot. Thus nouns, like verbs, have the five conjugations and the two paradigms.

Iroquois verbs have three moods, indicative, imperative, and subjunctive; and they have, in the indicative, seven tenses, the present, imperfect, perfect, pluperfect, aorist, future and paulo-post future. These moods and tenses are indicated either by changes of termination, or by prefixed particles, or by both conjoined. One authority makes six other tenses, but M. Cuoq prefers to include them among the special forms of the verb, of which mention will presently be made.

To give examples of these tenses, and the rules for their formation, would require more space than can be devoted to the subject in the present volume. The reader who desires to pursue the study is referred to the works of M. Cuoq already mentioned.

The verb takes a passive form by inserting the syllable at between the prefixed pronoun and the verb; and a reciprocal sense by inserting atat. Thus, kiatatas, I put in, katiatatas, I am put in; katatiatatas, I put myself in; konnis, I make; katonnis, I am made; katatonnis, I make myself. This syllable at is probably derived from the word oyata, body, which is used in the sense of "self," like the corresponding word hakey in the Delaware language.

The "transitions," or the pronominal forms which indicate the passage of the action of a transitive verb from the agent to the object, play an important part in the Iroquois language. In the Algonkin tongues these transitions are indicated partly by prefixed pronouns, and partly by terminal inflections. In the Iroquois the subjective and objective pronouns are both prefixed, as in French. In that language "il me voit" corresponds precisely with RAKAtkatos, "he-me-sees." Here the pronouns, ra, of the third person, and ka of the first, are evident enough. In other cases the two pronouns have been combined in a form which shows no clear trace of either of the simple pronouns; as in hetsenonwes, thou lovest him, and hianonwes, he loves thee. These combined pronouns are very numerous, and vary, like the simple pronouns, in the five conjugations.

The peculiar forms of the verb, analogous to the Semitic conjugations are very numerous. Much of the force and richness of the language depends on them. M. Cuoq enumerates-

1. The diminutive form, which affixes ha; as knekirhaHA, I drink a little; konkweHA (from onkwe, man), I am a man, but hardly one (i.e., I am a little of a man).

2. The augmentative, of which tsi is the affixed sign; as, knekirhaTSI, I drink much. This is sometimes lengthened to tsihon; as wakatonteTSIHON, I understand perfectly.

3 and 4. The cislocative, expressing motion towards the speaker, and the translocative, indicating motion tending from him. The former has t, the latter ie or ia, before the verb, as tasataweiat, come in; iasataweiat, go in.

5. The duplicative, which prefixes te, expresses an action which affects two or more agents or objects, as in betting, marrying, joining, separating. Thus, from ikiaks, I cut, we have tekiaks, I cut in two, where the prefix le corresponds to the Latin bi in "bisect." The same form is used in speaking of acts done by those organs of the body, such as the eyes and the hands, which nature has made double. Thus tekasenthos, I weep, is never used except in this form.

6. The reiterative is expressed by the sound of s prefixed to the verb. It sometimes replaces the cislocative sign; thus, tkahtenties, I come from yonder; skahtenties, I come again.

7. The motional is a form which by some is considered a special future tense. Thus, from khiatons, I write, we have khiatonnes, I am going to write; from katerios, I fight, katerioseres, I am going to the war; from kesaks, I seek, kesakhes, I am going to seek. These forms are irregular, and can only be learned by practice.

8. The causative suffix is tha; as from k'kowanen, I am great, we have k'kowanaTHA, I make great, I aggrandize. With at inserted we have a simulative or pretentious form, as katkowanaTHA, I make myself great, I pretend to be great. The same affix is used to give an instrumental sense; as from keriios, I kill, we have keriiohTHA, I kill him with such a weapon or instrument.

9. The progressive, which ends in tie (sometimes taking the forms atie, hatie, tatie), is much used to give the sense of becoming, proceeding, continuing, and the like; as wakhiatontie, I go on writing; wakatrorihatie, I keep on talking; wakeriwaientatie, I am attending to the business. The addition of an s to this form adds the idea of plurality or diversity of acts; thus, wakhiatonties, I go on writing at different times and places; wakatrorihaties, I keep on telling the thing, i.e., going from house to house.

10. The attributive has various forms, which can only be learned by practice or from the dictionaries. It expresses an action done for some other person; as, from wakiote, I work, we have kiotense, I work for some one; from katatis, I speak, katatiase, I speak in favor of some one.

11. The habitual ends in kon. From katontats, I hear, I consent, we have wakatontatskon, I am docile; from katatis, I speak, wakatatiatskon, I am talkative.

12. The frequentative has many forms, but usually ends in on, or ons. From khiatons, I write, we have in this form khiatonnions, I write many things; from katkahtos, I look, katkahtonnions, I look on all sides.

These are not all the forms of the Iroquois verb; but enough have been enumerated to give some idea of the wealth of the language in such derivatives, and the power of varied expression which it derives from this source.

The Iroquois has many particles which, like those of the Greek and French languages, help to give clearness to the style, though their precise meaning cannot always be gathered by one not perfectly familiar with the language. Ne and nene are frequently used as substitutes for the article and the relative pronouns. Onenh, now; kati, then, therefore; ok, nok, and neok, and; oni and neoni, also; toka and tokat, if, perhaps; tsi, when; kento, here; akwah, indeed, very; etho, thus, so; are, sometimes, again; ken, an interrogative particle, like the Latin ne--these and some others will be found in the Book of Rites, employed in the manner in which they are still used by the best speakers.

It must be understood that the foregoing sketch affords only the barest outline of the formation of the Iroquois language. As has been before remarked, a complete grammar of this speech, as full and minute as the best Sanscrit or Greek grammars, would probably equal and perhaps surpass those grammars in extent. The unconscious forces of memory and of discrimination required to maintain this complicated intellectual machine, and to preserve it constantly exact and in good working order, must be prodigious. Yet a comparison of Bruyas' work with the language of the present day shows that this purpose has been accomplished; and, what is still more remarkable, a comparison of the Iroquois with the Huron grammar shows that after a separation which must have exceeded five hundred years, and has probably covered twice that term, the two languages differ less from one another than the French of the twelfth century differed from the Italian, or than the Anglo-Saxon of King Alfred differed from the contemporary Low German speech. The forms of the Huron-Iroquois languages, numerous and complicated as they are, appear to be certainly not less persistent, and probably better maintained, than those of the written Aryan tongues.

ANCIENT RITES OF THE CONDOLING COUNCIL

ANCIENT RITES OF THE CONDOLING COUNCIL

OKAYONDONGHSERA YONDENNASE

OGHENTONH KARIGHWATEGHKWENH

DEYUGHNYONKWARAKTA, RATIYATS

1. Onenh weghniserade wakatyerenkowa desawennawenrate ne kenteyurhoton. Desahahishonne donwenghratstanyonne ne kentekaghronghwanyon. Tesatkaghtoghserontye ronatennossendonghkwe yonkwanikonghtaghkwenne, konyennetaghkwen. Ne katykenh nayoyaneratye ne sanikonra? Daghsatkaghthoghseronne ratiyanarenyon onkwaghsotsherashonkenhha; neok detkanoron ne shekonh ayuyenkwaroghthake jiratighrotonghkwakwe. Ne katykenh nayuyaneratye ne sanikonra desakaghserentonyonne?

2. Niyawehkowa katy nonwa onenh skennenji thisayatirhehon. Onenh nonwa oghseronnih denighroghkwayen. Hasekenh thiwakwekonh deyunennyatenyon nene konnerhonyon, "Ie henskerighwaghtonte." Kenyutnyonkwaratonnyon, neony kenyotdakarahon, neony kenkontifaghsoton. Nedens aesayatyenenghdon, konyennedaghkwen, neony kenkaghnekonyon nedens aesayatyenenghdon, konyennethaghkwen, neony kenwaseraketotanese kentewaghsatayenha kanonghsakdatye. Niyateweghnise rakeh yonkwakaronny; onidatkon yaghdekakonghsonde oghsonteraghkowa nedens aesayatyenenghdon, konyennethaghkwen.

ANCIENT RITES OF THE CONDOLING COUNCIL

THE PRELIMINARY CEREMONY

CALLED, "AT THE WOOD'S EDGE."

1. Now [1] to-day I have been greatly startled by your voice coming through the forest to this opening. You have come with troubled mind through all obstacles. You kept seeing the places where they met on whom we depended, my offspring. How then can your mind be at ease? You kept seeing the footmarks of our fore fathers; and all but perceptible is the smoke where they used to smoke the pipe together. Can then your mind be at ease when you are weeping on your way?

2. Great thanks now, therefore, that you have safely arrived. Now, then, let us smoke the pipe together. Because all around are hostile agencies which are each thinking, "I will frustrate their purpose." Here thorny ways, and here falling trees, and here wild beasts lying in ambush. Either by these you might have perished, my offspring, or, here by floods you might have been destroyed, my offspring, or by the uplifted hatchet in the dark outside the house. Every day these are wasting us; or deadly invisible disease might have destroyed you, my offspring.

3. Niyawenhkowa kady nonwa onenh skennenjy thadesarhadiyakonh. Hasekenh kanoron jinayawenhon nene aesahhahiyenenhon, nene ayakotyerenhon ayakawen, "Issy tyeyadakeron, akwah deyakonakorondon!" Ayakaweron oghnonnekenh niyuterenhhatye, ne konyennedaghkwen.

4. Rotirighwison onkwaghsotshera, ne ronenh, "Kenhenyondatsjistayenhaghse. Kendeyughnyonkwarakda eghtenyontatitenranyon orighokonha." Kensane yeshotiriwayen orighwakwekonh yatenkarighwentaseron, nene akwah denyontatyadoghseronko. Neony ne ronenh, "Ethononweh yenyontatenonshine, kanakdakwenniyukeh yenyontatideron."

5. Onenh kady iese seweryenghskwe sathaghyonnighshon:

Karhatyonni.
Oghskawaserenhon.
Gentiyo.
Onenyute.
Deserokenh.
Deghhodijinharakwenh.

---

[1] The paragraphs are not numbered in the original text. The numbers are prefixed in this work merely for convenience of reference.

The Iroquois Book of Rites

Oghrekyonny.
Deyuyewenton.

Etho ne niwa ne akotthaghyonnishon.

6. Onenh nene shehhawah deyakodarakeh ranyaghdenghshon:

Kaneghsadakeh.
Onkwehieyede.
Waghkerhon.
Kahhendohhon.
Dhogwenyoh.
Kayyhekwarakeh.

Etho ne niwa ne ranyaghdenshon.

3. Great thanks now, therefore, that in safety you have come through the forest. Because lamentable would have been the consequences had you perished by the way, and the startling word had come, "Yonder are lying bodies, yea, and of chiefs!" And they would have thought in dismay, what had happened, my offspring.

4. Our forefathers made the rule, and said, "Here they are to kindle a fire; here, at the edge of the woods, they are to condole with each other in few words." But they have referred thither [1] all business to be duly completed, as well as for the mutual embrace of condolence. And they said, "Thither shall they be led by the hand, and shall be placed on the principal seat."

5. Now, therefore, you who are our friends of the Wolf clan:

In John Buck's MS.	Supposed Meaning.
Ka rhe tyon ni.	The broad woods.
Ogh ska wa se ron hon.	Grown up to bushes again.
Gea di yo.	Beautiful plain.
De se ro ken.	Between two lines.
O nen yo deh.	Protruding stone.

---

[1] That is, to the Council House.

Te ho di jen ha ra kwen.	Two families in a long-house, one at each end.
Ogh re kyon ny.	(Doubtful.)
Te yo we yen don.	Drooping wings.

Such is the extent of the Wolf clan.

6. Now, then, thy children of the two clans of the Tortoise:

Ka ne sa da keh.	On the hill side.
Onkwi i ye de.	A person standing there.
Wegh ke rhon.	(Doubtful.)
Kah ken doh hon.	"
Tho gwen yoh.	"
Kah he kwa ke.	"

Such is the extent of the Tortoise clan.

7. Onenh nene jadadeken roskerewake:

Deyaokenh.
Jonondese.
Otskwirakeron.
Onaweron.

8. Onenh nene onghwa kehaghshonha:

Karhawenghradongh.
Karakenh.
Deyuhhero.
Deyughsweken.
Oxdenkeh.

Etho ne niwa roghskerewake.

Eghnikatarakeghne orighwakayongh.

9. Ne kaghyaton jinikawennakeh ne dewadadenonweronh, "ohhendonh karighwadeghkwenh" radiyats. Doka enyairon, "Konyennedaghkwen, onenh weghniserade yonkwatkennison. Rawenniyo raweghniseronnyh. Ne onwa konwende yonkwatkennison nene jiniyuneghrakwah jinisayadawen. Onenh onghwenjakonh niyonsakahhawe jinonweh nadekakaghneronnyonghkwe. Akwah kady okaghserakonh thadetyatroghkwanekenh.

10. "Onenh kady yakwenronh, wakwennyonkoghde okaghsery, akwah kady ok skennen thadenseghsatkaghthonnyonhheke.

11. "Nok ony kanekhere deyughsihharaonh ne sahondakon. Onenh kady watyakwaghsiharako waahkwadeweyendonh tsisaronkatah, kady nayawenh ne skennen thensathondeke enhtyewenninekenneh.

12. "Nok ony kanekhere deyughsihharaonh desanyatokenh. Onenh kady hone yakwenronh watyakwaghsihharanko, akwah kady ok skennen deghsewenninekenne dendewadatenonghweradon.

7. Now these thy brothers of the Bear clan:

De ya oken.	The Forks.
Jo non de seh.	It is a high hill.
Ots kwe ra ke ron.	Dry branches fallen to the ground.
Ogh na we ron.	The springs.

8. Now these have been added lately:

Ka rho wengh ra don.	Taken over the woods.
Ka ra ken.	White.
De yo he ro.	The place of flags (rushes).
De yo swe ken.	Outlet of the river.
Ox den ke.	To the old place.

Such is the extent of the Bear clan.

These were the clans in ancient times.

9. Thus are written the words of mutual greeting, called "the opening ceremony." Then one will say, "My offspring, now this day we are met together. God has appointed this day. Now, to-day, we are met together, on account of the solemn event which has befallen you. Now into the earth he has been conveyed to whom we have been wont to look. Yea, therefore, in tears let us smoke together.

10. "Now, then, we say, we wipe away the tears, so that in peace you may look about you.

11. "And, further, we suppose there is an obstruction in your ears. Now, then, we remove the obstruction carefully from your hearing, so that we trust you will easily hear the words spoken.

12. "And also we imagine there is an obstruction in your throat. Now, therefore, we say, we remove the obstruction, so that you may speak freely in our mutual greetings.

13. Onenh are oya, konyennethaghkwen. Nene kadon yuneghrakwah jinesadawen. Niyadeweghniserakeh sanekherenhonh ratikowanenghskwe. Onghwenjakonh niyeskahhaghs; ken-ony rodighskenrakeghdethaghkwe, ken-ony sanheghtyensera, ken-ony saderesera. Akwagh kady ok onek-wenghdarihengh thisennekwakenry.

14. Onenh kady yakwenronh wakwanekwenghdarokewanyon jisanakdade, ogh kady nenyawenne seweghniserathagh ne akwah ok skennen then kanakdiyuhake ji enghsitskodake denghsatkaghdonnyonheke.

15. Onenh nene Karenna,

    YONDONGHS "AIHAIGH."

Kayanerenh deskenonghweronne;
Kheyadawenh deskenonghweronne;
Oyenkondonh deskenonghweronne;
Wakonnyh deskenonghweronne.
Ronkeghsotah rotirighwane,--
Ronkeghsota jiyathondek.

16. Enskat ok enjerennokden nakwah oghnaken nyare enyonghdentyonko kanonghsakonghshon, enyairon:

17. "A-i Raxhottahyh! Onenh kajatthondek onenh enyontsdaren ne yetshiyadare! Ne ji onenh wakarighwakayonne ne sewarighwisahnonghkwe ne kayarenghkowah. Ayawenhenstokenghske daondayakotthondeke.

18. "Na-i Raxhottahyh! Ne kenne iesewenh enyakodenghthe nene noghnaken enyakaonkodaghkwe.

19. "Na-i Raxhottahyh! Onenh nonwa kathonghnonweh dhatkonkoghdaghkwanyon jidenghnonhon nitthatirighwayerathaghkwe."

13. "Now again another thing, my offspring. I have spoken of the solemn event which has befallen you. Every day you are losing your great men. They are being borne into the earth; also the warriors, and also your women, and also your grandchildren; so that in the midst of blood you are sitting.

14. "Now, therefore, we say, we wash off the blood marks from your seat, so that it may be for a time that happily the place will be clean where you are seated and looking around you."

15. Now the Hymn,

CALLED "HAIL."

I come again to greet and thank the League;
I come again to greet and thank the kindred;
I come again to greet and thank the warriors;
I come again to greet and thank the women.
My forefathers,--what they established,
My forefathers,--hearken to them!

16. The last verse is sung yet again, while he walks to and fro in the house, and says:

17. "Hail, my grandsires! Now hearken while your grandchildren cry mournfully to you,--because the Great League which you established has grown old. We hope that they may hear.

18. "Hail, my grandsires! You have said that sad will be the fate of those who come in the latter times.

19. "Oh, my grandsires! Even now I may have failed to perform this ceremony in the order in which they were wont to perform it."

20. "Na-i Raxhottahyh! Nene ji onenh wakarighwakayonne ne sewarighwisahnonghkwe, ne Kayarenghkowa. Yejisewatkonseraghkwanyon onghwenjakonshon yejisewayadakeron, sewarighwisahnhonkwe ne Kayanerenhkowah. Ne sanekenh ne seweghne aerengh niyenghhenwe enyurighwadatye Kayanerenghkowah."

21. Eghnikonh enyerighwawetharho kenthoh, are enjonderennoden enskat enjerenokden, onenh ethone enyakohetsde onenh are enjondentyonko kanonghsakonghshon, enyairon wahhy:

22. "A-i Raxhotthahyh! Onenh jatthondek kady nonwa jinihhotiyerenh,--orighwakwekonh natehaotiyadoreghtonh, nene roneronh ne enyononghsaghniratston. A-i Raxhotthahyh! nene ronenh: 'Onen nonwa wetewayennendane; wetewennakeraghdanyon; watidewennakarondonnyon.'

23. "Onenh are oya eghdeshotiyadoreghdonh, nene ronenh: 'Kenkisenh nenyawenne. Aghsonh thiyenjidewatyenghsaeke, onok enjonkwanekheren.' Nene ronenh: 'Kenkine nenyawenne. Aghsonh denyakokwanentonghsaeke, onok denjontadenakarondako. Nene doka ok yadayakonakarondatye onghwenjakonh niyaonsakahawe, A-i Raxhottahyh,' nene ronenh, 'da-edewenhheye onghteh, neok yadayakonakarondatye onghwenjakonh niyaonsakahawe.'

24. "Onenh are oya eghdeshodiyadoreghtonh, nai Raxhottahyh! Nene ronenh ne enyononghsaghniratston. Nene ronengh: 'Doka onwa kenenyondatyadawenghdate, ne kenkarenyakeghrondonhah ne nayakoghstonde ne nayeghnyasakenradake, ne kenh ne iesewenh, kenkine nenyawenne. Kendenyethirentyonnite kanhonghdakde dewaghsadayenhah.

20. "Oh, my grandsires! Even now that has become old which you established,--the Great League. You have it as a pillow under your heads in

the ground where you are lying,--this Great League which you established; although you said that far away in the future the Great League would endure."

21. So much is to be said here, and the Hymn is to be sung again, and then he is to go on and walk about in the house again, saying as follows:

22. "Hail, my grandsires! Now hear, therefore, what they did--all the rules they decided on, which they thought would strengthen the House. Hail, my grandsires! this they said: 'Now we have finished; we have performed the rites; we have put on the horns.'

23. "Now again another thing they considered, and this they said: 'Perhaps this will happen. Scarcely shall we have arrived at home when a loss will occur again.' They said, 'This, then, shall be done. As soon as he is dead, even then the horns shall be taken off For if invested with horns he should be borne into the grave,' oh, my grandsires, they said, 'we should perhaps all perish if invested with horns he is conveyed to the grave.'

24. "Then again another thing they determined, oh my grandsires! 'This,' they said, 'will strengthen the House.' They said, if any one should be murdered and [the body] be hidden away among fallen trees by reason of the neck being white, then you have said, this shall be done. We will place it by the wall in the shade.

25. "Onenh are oya eglidejisewayudoreghdonh, nene isewenh: 'Yahhonghdehdeyoyanere nene kenwedewayen, onwa enyeken nonkwade-resera; kadykenh niyakoghswathah, akwekonh nityakawenonhtonh ne kenyoteranentenyonhah. Enyonterenjiok kendonsayedane akwah enyakonewarontye, onok enyerighwanendon oghnikawenhonh ne kendeyerentyonny; katykenh nenyakorane nenyerighwanendon akare onenh enyakodokenghse. Onok na entkaghwadasehhon nakonikonra, onenh are ne eh enjonkwakaronny.'

26. "Onenh are oya eghdeshotiyadoreghdonh, nene ronenh: 'Kenkine nenyawenne. Endewaghneghdotako skarenhhesekowah, enwadonghwen-jadethare eghyendewasenghte tyoghnawatenghjihonh kathonghdeh thienkahhawe; onenh denghnon dentidewaghneghdoten, onenh denghnon yaghnonwendonh thiyaensayeken nonkwateresera.'

27. "Onenh are oya eghdeshotiyadoreghdonh, nene roneronh ne enyononghsaghniratston. Nene ronenh: 'Onenh wedewaweyennendane; wedewennakeraghdanyon. Doka nonkenh onghwajok onok enjonkwanekheren. Ken kady ne nenyawenne. Kenhendewaghnatatsherodarho ken kanakaryonniha deyunhonghdoyenghdongh yendewanaghsenghde, kennikanaghseshah, ne enyehharako ne kaneka akonikonghkahdeh. Enwadon ok jiyudakenrokde thadenyedane doghkara nentyewenninekenne enjondatenikonghketsko ne enyenikonglikwenghdarake. Onokna enjeyewendane yenjonthahida ne kayanerenghkowa.'

28. "Onenh kady ise jadakweniyu ken Kanonghsyonny, Dekanawidah, ne deghniwenniyu ne rohhawah Odadsheghte; onenh nene yeshodonnyh Wathadodarho; onenh nene yeshohowah akahenyonh; onare nene yeshodonnyh

25. "Now again you considered and you said: 'It is perhaps not well that we leave this here, lest it should be seen by our grandchildren; for they are troublesome, prying into every crevice. People will be startled at their returning in consternation, and will ask what has happened that this (corpse) is lying here; because they will keep on asking until they find it out. And they will at once be disturbed in mind, and that again will cause us trouble.'

26. "Now again they decided, and said: 'This shall be done. We will pull up a pine tree--a lofty tree--and will make a hole through the earth-crust, and will drop this thing into a swift current which will carry it out of sight, and then never will our grandchildren see it again.'

27. "Now again another thing they decided, and thought, this will strengthen the House. They said: 'Now we have finished; we have performed the rites. Perhaps presently it will happen that a loss will occur amongst us. Then this shall be done. We will suspend a pouch upon a pole, and will place in it some mourning wampum--some short strings--to be taken to the place where the loss was suffered. The bearer will enter, and will stand by the hearth, and will speak a few words to comfort those who will be mourning; and then they will be comforted, and will conform to the great law.'

28 Now, then, thou wert the principal of this Confederacy, Dekanawidah, with the joint principal, his son, Odadsheghte; and then again his uncle,

The Iroquois Book of Rites

Wathadodarho; and also again his son, Akahenyonh; and again his uncle, Kanyadariyu; onenh nene yeshonarase Shadekaronyes; onenh nene onghwa kehhaghsaonhah yejodenaghstahhere kanaghsdajikowah."

29. Onenh jatthondek sewarihwisaanonghkwe Kayarenhkowah. Onenh wakarighwakayonne. Onenh ne okne joskawayendon. Yetsisewanenyadanyon ne sewariwisaanonghkweh. Yejisewahhawihtonh, yetsisewennitskarahgwanyon; agwah neok ne skaendayendon. Etho yetsisewanonwadaryon. Sewarihwisaanonghkwe yetsisewahhawitonh. Yetsisewatgonseraghkwanyon sewarihwisaanonghkwe, Kayanerenhkowah.

30. Onenh kady jatthondek jadakweniyosaon sewarihwisaanonghkwe:

DEKARIHAOKENH!

Jatthontenyonk!
Jatagweniyosaon,
   AYONHWAHTHA!
Jatthontenyonk!
Jatagweniyosaon,
   SHATEKARIWATE!
Etho natejonhne!
Sewaterihwakhaonghkwe,
Sewarihwisaanonghkwe,
Kayanerenhkowah.

31. Jatthontenyonk!
Jatagweniyosaon,
   SHARENHAOWANE!
Jatthontenyonk!
Jatagweniyosaon,
   DEYONNHEHGONH!
Jatthontenyonk!
Jatagweniyosaon,

Kanyadariyu; and then again his cousin, Shadekaronyes; and then in later times additions were made to the great edifice."

29. Now listen, ye who established the Great League. Now it has become old. Now there is nothing but wilderness. Ye are in your graves who

established it. Ye have taken it with you, and have placed it under you, and there is nothing left but a desert. There ye have taken your intellects with you. What ye established ye have taken with you. Ye have placed under your heads what ye established--the Great League.

30. Now, then, hearken, ye who were rulers and founders:

    TEHKARIHHOKEN! [1]
Continue to listen!
Thou who wert ruler,
    HAYENWATHA!
Continue to listen!
Thou who wert ruler,
    SHADEKARIHWADE!
That was the roll of you,
You who were joined in the work,
You who completed the work,
The Great League.

31. Continue to listen!
Thou who wert ruler,
    SHARENHHOWANE!
Continue to listen!
Thou who wert ruler,
    TEHYONHEGHKWEN!
Continue to listen!
Thou who wert ruler,
    OGHRENREGOWAH!
Etho natejonhne!
Sewaterihwakhaonghkwe,
Sewarihwisaanonghkwe,
Kayanerenhkowah.

32. Jatthontenyonk!
Jatagweniyosaon,
    DEHENNAKARINE!
Jatthontenyonk!
Jatagweniyosaon,

---

[1] The names in this version are in the orthography of John Buck's MS.

The Iroquois Book of Rites

AGHSTAWENSERONTHA!
Jatthontenyonk!
Jatagweniyosaon,
   SHOSGOHAROWANE!
Etho natejonhne,
Sewatarihwakhaonghkwe,
Sewarihwisaanonghkwe,
Kayanerenhkowah.

33. Ise seniyatagweniyohkwe,
Jatathawhak.
Senirighwisaanonghkwe,
Kayanerenghkowah.
Ne deseniyenah;
Seninonsyonnitonh.
Onenh katy jatthontenyonk
Jatakweniyosaon,
   ODATSEGHTE!
Jatthontenyonk!
Jatakweniyosaon,
   KANONHGWENYODON!
Jatthontenyonk!
Jatakweniyosaon,
   DEYOHHAGWENTE!
Etho natejonhne!
Sewaterihwakhaonghkwe.
Sewarihwisaanonghkwe,
Kayanerenhkowah.
   OWENHEGHKOHNA!
That was the roll of you,
You who were joined in the work,
You who completed the work,
The Great League.

32. Continue to listen!
Thou who wert ruler,
   TEHHENNAGHKARIHNE!
Continue to listen!
Thou who wert ruler,
   AGHSTAWENSERONTTHA!

Continue to listen!
Thou who wert ruler,
   SHAGHSKOHAROWANE!
That was the roll of you,
You who were joined in the work,
You who completed the work,
The Great League.

33. Ye two were principals,
Father and son,
Ye two completed the work,
The Great League.
Ye two aided each other,
Ye two founded the House.
Now, therefore, hearken!
Thou who wert ruler,
   ODATSEGHDEH!
Continue to listen!
Thou who wert ruler,
   KAHNONKWENYAH!
Continue to listen!
Thou who wert ruler,
   TEHYOHHAKWENDEH!
That was the roll of you,
You who were joined in the work,
You who completed the work,
The Great League.

34. Jatthontenyonk!
Jatakweniyosaon,
   SHONONSESE!
Jatthontenyonk!
Jatakweniyosaon,
   DAONAHROKENAGH!
Jatthontenyonk!
Jatakweniyosaon,
   ATYATONNENHTHA!
Etho natejonhne!
Sewaterihwakhaonghkwe,
Sewarihwisaanonghkwe,

Kayanerenhkowah.

35. Jatthontenyonk!
Jatakweniyosaon,
    DEWATAHONHTENYONK!
Jatthontenyonk!
Jatakweniyosaon,
    KANIYATAHSHAYONK!
Jatthontenyonk!
Jatakweniyosaon,
    ONWATSATONHONH!
Etho natejonhne!
Sewaterihwakhaonghkwe,
Sewarihwisaanonghkwe,
Kayanerenhkowah.

36. Eghyesaotonnihsen:
Onenh jatthontenyonk!
Jatakweniyosaon,
    THATOTARHO!
Jatthontenyonk!
Etho ronarasehsen:
Jatakweniyosaon,
    ENNESERARENH!
Jatthontenyonk!
Jatakweniyosaon,

34. Continue to listen!
Thou who wert ruler,
    SHONONGHSESEH!
Continue to listen!
Thou who wert ruler,
    THONAEGHKENAH!
Continue to listen!
Thou who wert ruler,
    HAHTYADONNENTHA!
That was the roll of you,
You who were joined in the work,
You who completed the work,
The Great League.

35. Continue to listen!
Thou who wert ruler,
    TEHWAHTAHONTENYONK!
Continue to listen!
Thou who wert ruler,
    KAHNYADAGHSHAYEN!
Continue to listen!
Thou who wert ruler,
    HONWATSHADONNEH!
That was the roll of you,
You who were joined in the work,
You who completed the work,
The great League.

36. These were his uncles:
Now hearken!
Thou who wert ruler,
    WATHADOTARHO:
Continue to listen!
These were the cousins
Thou who wert ruler,
    ONEHSEAGHHEN!
Continue to listen!
Thou who wert ruler,
    DEHATKAHTHOS!
Jatthontenyonk!
Waghontenhnonterontye.
Jatakweniyosaon,
    ONYATAJIWAK!
Jatthontenyonk!
Jatakweniyosaon,
    AWEKENYADE!
Jatthontenyonk!
Jatakweniyosaon,
    DEHAYADKWARAYEN!
Etho natejonhne!

37. Yeshohawak:
Rokwahhokowah.

The Iroquois Book of Rites

Etho kakeghrondakwe
Ne kanikonghrashon,
   RONONGHWIREGHTONH!
Etho natejonhne!

38. Etho yeshotonnyh,
Tekadarakehne.
   KAWENENSERONDON!
   HAGHRIRON!
Etho nadehhadihne!
39. Wahhondennonterontye,
   RONYENNYENNIH!
   SHODAKWARASHONH!
   SHAKOKENGHNE!
Etho nadejonhne!

40. Etho niyawenonh,
Karihwakayonh.
Shihonadewiraratye,
Tehhodidarakeh.
Rakowanenh,
   TEHHATKAHDONS!
Continue to listen!
These were as brothers thenceforth:
Thou who wert ruler,
   SKANIADAJIWAK:
Continue to listen!
Thou who wert ruler,
   AWEAKENYAT!
Continue to listen!
Thou who wert ruler,
   TEHAYATKWAYEN!
That was the roll of you!

37. Then his son:
He is the great Wolf.
There were combined
The many minds!
   HONONWIREHDONH!
That was the roll of you.

38. These were his uncles,
Of the two clans:
   KAWENENSEAGHTONH!
   HAHHIHHONH!
That was the roll of them!

39. These were as brothers thenceforth
   HOHYUNHNYENNIH!
   SHOTEHGWASEH!
   SHAHKOHKENNEH!
This was the roll of you.

40. This befell
In ancient times.
They had their children,
Those the two clans.
He the high chief,
   RASERHAGHRHONK!
Etho wahhoronghyaronnyon:
Roghskenrakeghdekowah,
Rakowanenh,
Tehhotyatakarorenh,
   SKANAWADYH!
Etho natejonhne!

41. Yeshohhawak,
   TEKAHENYONK:
Yeshonadadekenah:
   JINONTAWERAON!
Etho natejonhne!

42.   KADAKWARASONH!
   SHOYONWESE!
   ATYASERONNE!
Etho natejonhneh!

43, Yeshondadekenah,
   TEYORONGHYONKEH!
   TEYODHOREGHKONH!

The Iroquois Book of Rites

WATHYAWENHETHON!
Etho natejonhne!

44. ATONTARAHERHA!
    TESKAHE!
Etho natejonhneh!

45. Yeshotonnyh,
    SKANYADARIYO!
Yeshonaraseshen,
    SHADEKARONYES!
Etho natejonhneh!

46. SATYENAWAT!
Yeshonaraseshen,
    SHAKENJOWANE!
Etho natejonhneh!
    SAHHAHWIH!
This put away the clouds:
He was a war chief;
He was a high chief--
Acting in either office:
    SKAHNAHWAHTIH!
This was the roll of you!

41. Then his son,
    TAHKAHENHYUNH!
With his brother,
    JIHNONTAHWEHHEH.
This was the roll of you!

42. KAHTAHGWAHJIH!
    SHONYUNHWESH!
    HAHTYAHSENHNEH!
This was the roll of you!

43. Then they who are brothers:
    TEHYUHENHYUNHKOH!
    TEHYUHTOHWEHGWIH!
    TYAWENHHEHTHONH!

This was the roll of you.

44. HAHTONHTAHHEHHAH!
    TESHKAHHEA!
This was the roll of you!

45. Then his uncle,
    SKAHNYAHTEIHYUH!
With his cousin,
    SHAHTEHKAHENHYESH.
This was the roll of you!

46. SATYEHNAHWAHT!
With his cousin,
    SHAKENHJOHNAN!
This was the roll of you!

47. KANOKARIH!
Yeshonarase,--onwa
    NISHARYENEN!
Etho natejonhneh!

48. Onghwa keghaghshonah
Yodenaghstahhere
Kanaghstajikowah.
Yatehhotihohhataghkwen.
Etho ronaraseshen,
Yadehninhohhanonghne:
    KANONGHKERIDAWYH!
Yeshonaraseshen,
    TEYONINHOKARAWENH!
Etho natejonhneh!

49. Onenh watyonkwentendane
Kanikonrakeh.

47. KAHNOHKAIH!
With his cousin,--then
    NISHAHYEHNENHHAH!
This was the roll of you!

48. Then, in later times,
They made additions
To the great mansion.
These were at the doorway,
They who were cousins,
These two guarded the doorway:
   KANONHKEHIHTAWIH!
With his cousin,
   TYUHNINHOHKAWENH!
This was the roll of you!

49. Now we are dejected
In our minds.

THE BOOK OF THE YOUNGER NATIONS.

(ONONDAGA DIALECT.)

1. a. Yo o-nen o-nen wen-ni-sr-te o-nen wa-ge-ho-gar-a-nyat ne-tha-non-ni-sr-son-tar-yen na-ya-ne o-shon-tar-gon-go-nar nen-tis-no-war-yen na-ye-ti-na gar-weear-har-tye ne swih-ar-gen-ahr ne-tho-se hen-ga-ho-gar-a-nyat nen-tha-o-ta-gen-he-tak ne-tho-har-ten-gar-ton-ji-yar-hon-on nar-ye-en-gwa-wen-ne-kentar ne-ten-gon-nen-tar-hen na-a-yen-tar.

1. b. Tar onen na-on-gen shis-gis-war-tha-en-ton-tye-na on-gwr-non-sen-shen-tar-qua nar-te-har-yar-ar-qui-nar-nan-gar-wen-ne-srh-ha-yo-ton-har-tye nen-gar-nen-ar-ta ho-ti-sgen-ar-ga-tar nen-o-ne gar-nen-ar-ti kon-hon-wi-sats-nen-o-ni tar-ga-non-tye na on-quar-sat-har nen-o hon-tar-gen-hi-se-non-tye nen-o wen-gr-ge go-yar-da-nen-tar-hon nen-tho nr-ta-war ta-har-yar-ar-qui-nar nen-gar-wen-ne-sar han-yo-ton-hr-tye tar o-nen-ti tya-quar-wen-ne-gen-har nen-a-shen ne-yar-quar-tar-ta-gen.

1. c. O-nen-ti-a-wen-hen nar-ya-he-yr-genh thar-ne-ho-ti-e-quar-te nen-on-quar-noh-shen-ta-qua nen-o on-qua-jas-harn-ta-qua nar-ye-gen-na-ho-nen nar-ye-na te-was-hen nen-ne-gon-hi-war na-tho na-ho-te-yen-nen-tar-e tar-day-was-shen nen-ne-yo-ewa na-ar-wen-ha-yo-dar-ge nen-on-quar-twen-non-ty o-nen en-hen-wa-yar-shon nen-na-tho-on-ne-yar-quar-ya-ar nen-a-shen ne-yar-quar-tar-te-ken.

1. d. On-en-ti-eh-o-yar nen-ton-ta-yar-quar-wen-ni-ken-ar-nar-ya-hi-yar-gen na-ar-quar-ton sis-jih-wa-tha-en-ton-tye-o-yar-na son-quar-yo-ten-se-nar tar-nr-ye-ti-na hon-sar-ho-har-we-ti-har-tye

THE BOOK OF THE YOUNGER NATIONS.

(TRANSLATION.)

1. a. Now--now this day--now I come to your door where you are mourning in great darkness, prostrate with grief. For this reason we have come here

The Iroquois Book of Rites

to mourn with you. I will enter your door, and come before the ashes and mourn with you there; and I will speak these words to comfort you.

1. b. Now our uncle has passed away, he who used to work for all, that they might see the brighter days to come,--for the whole body of warriors and also for the whole body of women, and also the children that were running around, and also for the little ones creeping on the ground, and also those that are tied to the cradle-boards: for all these he used to work that they might see the bright days to come. This we say, we three brothers.

1. c. Now the ancient lawgivers have declared--our uncles that are gone, and also our elder brothers--they have said, it is worth twenty--it was valued at twenty--and this was the price of the one who is dead. And we put our words on it (i. e. the wampum), and they recall his name--the one that is dead. This we say and do, we three brothers.

1. d. Now there is another thing we say, we younger brothers. He who has worked for us has gone afar off; and he also will in time take with him all these—the nen-qr-nen-hr-te ho-ti-sken-ar-ga-tar nen-o-ne gar-nen-har-te gon-thon-we-sas on-sar-ho-na-tar-que-har-tye nar-ya-har-tes-gar-no-wen na o-nen na-en-gar-ya-tye-nen-har nen-war-thon-wi-sas ar-ques-sis-jit nar-te-yo-nen-ha-ase en-war-nten-har-wat-tha nen-on-quar-ta-shar o-nen o-yar-nen-eh-te-ge-non-tyes on-quar-te-shar nr-ya-o-ne sar-o-har-we-ti-har-tye o-nen o-yar nens-o-ni-ta-gen-hi-se-non-tyes o-wen-gar-ge ga-yr-tr-nen-tak-hon ne-tho nr-te-war on-sar-ho-har-we-ti-har-tye.

1. e. O-nen ty-a on-yar ta-ya-quar-wen-ne-ken-har nen-a-sen ne-yar-quar-tar-te-gen o-nen-ty ton-tar-wen-ten-eh nen-o-nen thon-tar-yar-tyar-ton-tye nen-wa-gon-yon-wen-jar-nan-har tar-o-nen ha-o-yar nen-ta-yo-quar wen ne-ken-e-har-tye. O-nen-te-ar-wen-han o-nen war-quar-de-yen-non-nyar-hen na-shar-non-wa nr-o-tas-are-quar-hen-ten o-nen wa-tya-quar-ha-tar-wen-ya-hon nen-ar o-ar-shon-ar nen-tar-yon-quar-ty ne-tho hon-ne-yar-quar-ya-ar nen-ar-shen ne-yar-quar-ta-te-kenh.

2. O-nen-ti-eh-o-yar nen-ton-tar-yar-quar-wen-ne-ken-har nen-o-son-tar-gon-go-nar nen-ti-sno-war-gen. O-nen-ti ton-sar-gon-en-nya-eh-tha ar-guas hi-yar-ga-tha te-jo-ge-grar O-nen-ti sar-gon-ar-gwar-nen-tak-ten sken-nen-gink-ty then-skar-ar-tayk O-nen en-gar-ar-qui-ken-nha ne-tho tens-shar-ar-tyen. O-nen yo-nen-tyon-ha-tye. Ar-ghwas ten-yo-ten-har-en-ton-nyon-ne.

Ne-tho tens-gar-ar-tye a-ghwas sken-non-jis ten-yo-yar-neh ne onen en-gr-ar-gwen-har o-ty-nen-yar-wen-har hen-jo-har-ten-har sar-ne-gon are. Ne-tho han-ne-yar-gwar-ya-ar nen-ar-sen ne-yar-quar-tr-ta-gen.

3. O-nen-ti-eh-o-yar nen-ton-ta-yar-quar-wen-ne-ken-har. O-nen-nen-ti war-tyar-war-see-har-an-qua te-shar-hon-tar-gar-en-tar nen-they-yon-tar-ge-har-te nen-te-sar-nar-ton-ken whole body of warriors and also the whole body of women--they will go with him. But it is still harder when the woman shall die, because with her the line is lost. And also the grandchildren and the little ones who are running around--these he will take away; and also those that are creeping on the ground, and also those that are on the cradle-boards; all these he will take away with him.

1. e. Now then another thing we will say, we three brothers. Now you must feel for us; for we came here of our own good-will--came to your door that we might say this. And we will say that we will try to do you good. When the grave has been made, we will make it still better. We will adorn it, and cover it with moss. We will do this, we three brothers.

2. Now another thing we will say, we younger brothers. You are mourning in the deep darkness. I will make the sky clear for you, so that you will not see a cloud. And also I will give the sun to shine upon you, so that you can look upon it peacefully when it goes down. You shall see it when it is going. Yea! the sun shall seem to be hanging just over you, and you shall look upon it peacefully as it goes down. Now I have hope that you will yet see the pleasant days. This we say and do, we three brothers.

3. Now then another thing we say, we younger brothers. Now we will open your ears, and also your throat, for there is something that has been choking you hon-ne-ty ar-war-na-gen-tar wen-jar-wa-gar-ha-e nar-ya-har ten-skar-har-we-tar-han nen-o-ge-gwr-en-yone nen-tye-sar-nar-ton-ken o-ty-nen-yar-wen-har nen-en-jo-har-ten-ar sar-ne-gon-are ne-tho hon-ne-yar-war-ya-ar nen-a-sen ne-yar-quar-tar-te-kenh.

4. O-nen-ti-eh-o-yar nen-ton-tar-yr-quar-wen-ne-ken-tye hon-nen ton-sar-war-kon-ha-jar-ha-jan nen-they-gar-kon-ha-shon-ton-har-tye hon-nen-ti nen-sar-kon-ge-ter-yen-has hon-nen-oni nen-ton-sar-gon-nen-ha-tieh o-nen o-tieh-nen-yar-wen-har nen-en-jo-har-tyen-har sar-ne-gon-are ne-tho hon-ne-yar-quar-yar-ar nen-a-sen ne-yar-qwr-tar-te-kenh.

5. O-nen-ti-eh-o-yar nen-ton-tar-yar-qwar-wen-ne-ken-har nar-ya-ti-ar-wen-han nen-tar-ehe-tar-nen-jar-tar-ti-war-ten nen-ton-gar-ke-sen nen-na-hon-yar-na on-har-wen-ne-gen-tar nar-ya-na sar-hon-ta-je-wants as-kar-we ar-san-nen-sen-wen-hat ne-tho o-ni -nen-yar-wen-hon-sken-are-gen-tar hor-go-war-nen-nen-hon-yar-na an-har-wen-ne-gen-tar are-we ar-sen-nen-sun-sar-wen-hat ne-tho on-ne-yar-quar-ya-ar nen-ar-sen ne-yr-qwar-tr-ta-kenh.

6. O-nen-ti-eh-o-yar nen-ton-tar-yar-quar-wen-ne-ken-hr nar-ye-ti-na-ar-wen-han nen-an-har-ya-tye-nen-har nen-na-hon-yar-na nr-ya-ti-nar nen-ne-yo-sar-tar ken-yar-tar nen-ji-gar-han nen-ta-hon-gren-tar wi-nar-na-ge-ne-yo-snon-wa nen-o-yar-en-sar-tyar-tar-nyar-ten a-ren ne-tho one-yar-qwar-yaar nen-ar-sen ne-yr-quar-tar-te-kenh.

7. O-nen-ti-eh-o-yar nen-ton-tr-yar-quar-wen-ne-ken-har nr-ya-ti-ar-wen-han sar-gon-nr-tar-eh-ya-tars nen-gr-nr-gar-yon-ne-ta-ar nen-jar-ne-qr-nar-sis-ah nen ne-tho war-ar-guar-sins-tar na-tho-ti-an-sar-wa nen-thon-gr-gey-san e-his-an-skas-gen-nen one-ha-yat nen-war-o-yan-quar-a-ton-on-tye nen-yar-gar-ker ta-gr-nr-squaw-ya-an-ne ne-tho on-ne-yar-quar-ya-ar nen-ar-sen ne-yar-quar-ta-te-kenh.

7. b. Tar-o-nen sar-gon-yan-nen-tar-ah tar-o-nen-ti ton-tar-ken-yar-tas. and we will also give you the water that shall wash down all the troubles in your throat. We shall hope that after this your mind will recover its cheerfulness. This we say and do, we three brothers.

4. Now then there is another thing we say, we younger brothers. We will now remake the fire, and cause it to burn again. And now you can go out before the people, and go on with your duties and your labors for the people. This we say and do, we three brothers.

5. Now also another thing we say, we younger brothers. You must converse with your nephews; and if they say what is good, you must listen to it. Do not cast it aside. And also if the warriors should say any thing that is good, do not reject it. This we say, we three brothers.

6. Now then another thing we say, we younger brothers. If any one should fall--it may be a principal chief will fall and descend into the grave--then the horns shall be left on the grave, and as soon as possible another shall be put in his place. This we say, we three brothers.

7. Now another thing we say, we younger brothers. We will gird the belt on you, with the pouch, and the next death will receive the pouch, whenever you shall know that there is death among us, when the fire is made and the smoke is rising. This we say and do, we three brothers.

7. b. Now I have finished. Now show me the man! [1]

---

[1] i.e., "Point out to me the man whom I am to proclaim as chief, in place of the deceased."

NOTES ON THE CANIENGA BOOK

THE meaning of the general title, Okayondonghsera Yondennase, has been already explained (Introduction, p. 48). In the sub-title, the word oghentonh is properly an adverb, meaning firstly, or foremost. This title might, be literally rendered, "First the ceremony, 'At-the-wood's-edge' they call it."

1. The chiefs, in their journey to the place of meeting, are supposed to have passed the sites of many deserted towns, in which councils had formerly been held. Owing to the frequent removals of their villages, such deserted sites were common in the Iroquois country. The speaker who welcomes the arriving guests supposes that the view of these places had awakened in their minds mournful recollections.

Desawennawenrate,--"thy voice coming over." This word is explained in the Glossary. It is in the singular number. According to the Indian custom, the speaker regards himself as representing the whole party for whom he speaks, and he addresses the leader of the other party as the representative and embodiment of all who come with him. Throughout the speeches "I" and "thou" are used in the well under stood sense of "we" and "ye." In like manner, tribes and nations are, as it were, personified. A chief, speaking for the Onondagas, will say, "I (that is, my nation) am angry; thou (the Delaware people) hast done wrong." This style of bold personification is common in the scriptures. Moses warns the Israelites: "Thou art a stiff-necked people." "Oh my people!" exclaims Isaiah; "they which lead thee cause thee to err."

2. Denighroghkwayen, "let us two smoke." This word is in the dual number, the two parties, the hosts and the guests, being each regarded as one individual.

The difficulties and dangers which in the early days of the confederacy beset the traveler in threading his way through the forest, from one Indian nation to another, are vividly described in this section. The words are still employed by their speakers as an established form, though they have ceased to have any pertinence to their present circumstances.

3. Akwah deyakonakarondon, "yea, of chiefs,"--literally, "yea, having horns." The custom of wearing horns as part of the head-dress of a chief has been long disused among the Iroquois; but the idiom remains in the language, and the horns, in common parlance, indicate the chief, as the coronet suggests the nobleman in England. Among the western Indians, as is well known, the usage still survives. "No one," says Catlin, "wears the head-dress surmounted with horns except the dignitaries who are very high in authority, and whose exceeding valor, worth, and power are admitted by all." These insignia of rank are, he adds, only worn on special and rare occasions, as in meeting embassies, or at warlike parades or other public festivals, or sometimes when a chief sees fit to lead a war-party to battle. [1] The origin of the custom is readily understood. The sight, frequent enough in former days, of an antlered stag leading a herd of deer would be quite sufficient to suggest to the quick apprehension of the Indian this emblem of authority and pre-eminence.

5. Sathaghyonnighson, "thou who art of the Wolf clan." The clan is addressed in the singular number, as one person. It is deserving of notice that the titles of clanship used in the language of ceremony are not derived from the ordinary names of the animals which give the clans their designations. Okwaho is wolf, but a man of the Wolf clan is called Tahionni,--or, as written in the text, Taghyonni. In ordinary speech, however, the expression rokwaho, "he is a Wolf," might be used.

The English renderings of the names in the list of towns are those which the interpreters finally decided upon. In several instances they doubted about the meaning, and in some cases they could not suggest an explanation. Either the words are obsolete, or they have come down in such a corrupt form that their original elements and purport cannot be determined. As regards the sites of the towns, see the Appendix, Note E.

6. Deyakodarakeh ranyaghdenghshon,--"the two clans of the Tortoise." Respecting the two sub-gentes into which the Tortoise clan was divided, see ante, p. 53. Anowara is the word for tortoise, but raniahten (or, in the

---

[1] Letters and Notes on the Manners, Customs, and Condition of the North American Indians. By George Catlin; p. 172.

orthography of the text, ranyaghdengh) signifies, "he is of the Tortoise clan."

7. Jadadeken roskerewake, thy brother of the Bear clan." Okwari is bear, but roskerewake signifies "he is of the Bear clan." Rokwari, "he is a Bear," might, however, be used with the same meaning.

8. Onghwa kehaghshonha, "now recently." It is possible that onghwa is here written by mistake for orighwa. The word orighwakayongh, which immediately follows, signifies "in ancient times," and the corresponding word orighwakehaghshonha would be "in younger times." The period in which these additions were made, though styled recent, was probably long past when the "Book of Rites" was committed to writing; otherwise many towns which are known to have existed at the latter date would have been added to the list. In fact, the words with which the catalogue of towns closes "these were the clans in ancient times,"--seem to refer these later additions, along with the rest, back to a primitive era of the confederacy.

9. Rawenniyo raweghniseronnyh, "God has appointed this day," or, literally, "God makes this day." In these words are probably found the only trace of any modification of the Book of Rites caused by the influence of the white visitors and teachers of the modern Iroquois. As the very fact that the book was written in the alphabet introduced by the missionaries makes us certain that the person who reduced it to writing had been under missionary instruction, it might be deemed surprising that more evidences of this influence are not apparent. It is probable, however, that the conservative feeling of the Council would have rejected any serious alterations in their ancient forms. It seems not unlikely that David of Schoharie--or whoever was the penman on this occasion--may have submitted his work to his missionary teacher, and that in deference to his suggestion a single interpolation of a religious cast, to which no particular objection could be made, was allowed to pass.

The word Rawenniyo, as is well known, is the term for God which was adopted by the Catholic missionaries. It is, indeed, of Huron-Iroquois origin, and may doubtless have been occasionally employed from the earliest times as an epithet proper for a great divinity. Its origin and precise meaning are explained in the Appendix, Note B. The Catholic missionaries appropriated it as the special name of the Deity, and its use in later times is probably to be regarded as an evidence of Christian influence. That the sentence in which it occurs in the text is probably an interpolation, is shown by the fact that the words which precede this sentence are repeated, with a slight change, immediately after it. Having interjected this pious expression, the writer seems to have thought it necessary to resume the thread of the discourse by going back to the phrase which had preceded it. It will be observed that the religious sentiment proper to the Book of Rites appears to be confined to expressions of reverence for the great departed, the founders of the commonwealth. This circumstance, however, should not be regarded as indicating that the people were devoid of devotional feeling of another kind. Their frequent "thanksgiving festivals" afford sufficient evidence of the strength of this sentiment; but they apparently considered its display out of place in their political acts.

15. Nene karenna, "the song," or "hymn." The purport of this composition is explained in the Introduction (ante, p. 62). Before the Book of Rites came into my possession I had often heard the hymn repeated, or sung, by different individuals, in slightly varying forms. The Onondaga version, given me on the Syracuse Reservation, contains a line,--Negwiyage teskenonhenhne," which is not found in the Canienga MS. It is rendered "I come to greet the children." The affection of the Indians for their children, which is exhibited in various passages of the Book, is most apparent in the Onondaga portion.

Kayanerenh. This word is variously rendered,--"the peace," "the law," and "the league," (see ante, p. 33) Here it evidently stands for Kayanerenhkowa, "the Great Peace," which is the name usually given by the Kanonsionni to their league, or federal constitution.

Deskenonghweronne, or in the modern French orthography, teskenonhweronne, "we come to greet and thank," is a good example of the comprehensive force of the Iroquois tongue. Its root is nonhwe, or nonwe, which is found in kenonhwes, I love, like, am pleased with--the initial syllable ke being the first personal pronoun. In the frequentative form this becomes kenonhweron, which has the meaning of "I salute and thank," i.e., I manifest by repeated acts my liking or gratification. The s prefixed to this word is the sign of the reiterative form: skenonhweron, "again I greet and thank." The terminal syllable ne and the prefixed te are respectively the signs of the motional and the cislocative forms,--"I come hither again to greet and thank." A word of six syllables, easily pronounced (and in the Onondaga dialect reduced to five) expresses fully and forcibly the meaning for which eight not very euphonious English words are required. The notion that the existence of these comprehensive words in an Indian language, or any other, is an evidence of deficiency in analytic power, is a fallacy which was long ago exposed by the clear and penetrative reasoning of Duponceau, the true father of American philology.[1] As he has well explained, analysis must precede synthesis. In fact, the power of what may be termed analytic synthesis,--the mental power which first resolves words or things into their elements, and then puts them together in new forms,--is a creative or co-ordinating force, indicative of a higher natural capacity than the act of mere analysis. The genius which framed the word teskenonhweronne is the same that, working with other elements, produced the steam-engine and the telephone.

Ronkeghsota jiyathondek. Two translations of this verse were given by different interpreters. One made it an address to the people: "My forefathers--hearken to them!" i.e., listen to the words of our forefathers, which I am about to repeat. The other considered the verse an invocation to the ancestors themselves. "My forefathers! hearken ye!" The words will bear either rendering, and either will be consonant with the speeches which follow.

The lines of this hymn have been thus cast into the metre of Longfellow's "Hiawatha:"--

"To the great Peace bring we greeting
To the dead chiefs kindred, greeting
To the warriors round him, greeting
To the mourning women, greeting!
These our grandsires' words repeating,
Graciously, O grandsires, hear us!"

16. Enyonghdentyonko kanonghsakonghshon,--"to and fro in the house." In councils and formal receptions, it is customary for the orator to walk slowly to and fro during the intervals of his speech. Sometimes, before beginning his address, he makes a circuit of the assembly with a meditative aspect, as if collecting his thoughts. All public acts of the Indians are marked with some sign of deliberation.

---

[1] See the admirable Preface to his translation of Zeisberger's Delaware Grammar, p. 94.

21. Eghnikonh enyerighwawetharho kenthoh,--" thus they will close the ceremony here." The address to the forefathers, which is mainly an outburst of lamentation over the degeneracy of the times, is here concluded. It would seem, from what follows, that at this point the candidate for senatorial honors is presented to the council, and is formally received among them, with the usual ceremonies, which were too well known to need description. The hymn is then sung again, and the orator proceeds to recite the ancient laws which the founders of their confederacy established.

22. Watidewennakarondonnyon, "we have put on the horns in other words, "we have invested the new chief with the ensigns of office,"--or, more briefly, "we have installed him." The latter is the meaning as at present understood; but it is probable that, in earlier days, the panoply of horns was really placed on the head of the newly inducted councillor.

23. Aghsonh denyakokwanentonghsaeke, etc., "as soon as he is dead" (or, according to another rendering, "when he is just dying") the horns shall be taken off. The purport and object of this law are set forth in the Introduction, p. 67.

24. Ne nayakoghstonde ne nayeghnyasakenradake, "by reason of the neck being white." The law prescribed in this section to govern the proceedings of the Council in the case of homicide has been explained in the Introduction, p. 63. The words now quoted, however, introduce a perplexity which cannot be satisfactorily cleared up. The aged chief, John S. Johnson, when asked their meaning, was only able to say that neither he nor his fellow-councillors fully understood it. They repeated in council the words as they were written in the book, but in this case, as in some others, they were not sure of the precise significance or purpose of what they said. Some of them thought that their ancestors, the founders, had foreseen the coming of the white people, and wished to advise their successors against quarreling with their future neighbors. If this injunction was really implied in the words, we must suppose that they were an interpolation of the Christian chief, David of Schoharie, or possibly of his friend Brant. They do not, however, seem to be, by any means, well adapted to convey this meaning. The probability is that they are a modern corruption of some earlier phrase, whose meaning had become obsolete. They are repeated by the chiefs in council, as some antiquated words in the authorized version of the scriptures are read in our

The Iroquois Book of Rites

own churches, with no clear comprehension--perhaps with a total misconception--of their original sense.

27. Enjonkwanekheren, "we shall lose some one," or, more literally, we shall fail to know some person. This law, which is fully explained in the Introduction, p. 70, will be found aptly exemplified in the Onondaga portion of the text, where the speeches of the "younger brothers" are evidently framed in strict compliance with the injunctions here given.

28. Jadakweniyu. This word, usually rendered "ruler," appears to mean "principal person," or perhaps originally a "very powerful person." It is a compound word, formed apparently from oyata, body or person, kakwennion, to be able, and the adjective termination iyu or iyo, in its original sense of "great." (See Appendix, Note B.) M. Cuoq, in his Iroquois Lexicon, defines the verb kiatakwenniyo as meaning "to be the important personage, the first, the principal, the president." It corresponds very nearly to the Latin princeps, and, as applied in the following litany to the fifty great hereditary chiefs of the Iroquois, might fairly enough be rendered "prince."

Kanonghsyonny, in modern orthography, Kanonsionni. For the origin and meaning of this word, and an explanation of the following section, see the Introduction, p. 75.

Yejodenaghstahhere kanaghsdajikowah, lit., "they added frame-poles to the great framework." Each of these com pounds comprises the word kanaghsta, which is spelt by Bruyas, gannasta, and defined by him, "poles for making a cabin,--the inner one, which is bent to form the frame of a cabin." The reference in these words is to the Tuscaroras, Tuteloes, Nanticokes, and other tribes, who were admitted into the confederacy after its first formation. From a manuscript book, written in the Onondaga dialect, which I found at "Onondaga Castle," in September, 1880, I copied a list of the fifty councillors, which closed with the words, "shotinastasonta kanastajikona Ontaskaeken,"--literally, "they added a frame-pole to the great framework, the Tuscarora nation."

29. Onenh jathondek, sewarihwisaanonghkwe Kayanerenghkowa,--"now listen, ye who completed the work, the Great League." This section, though written continuously as prose, was probably always sung, like the list of chiefs which follows. It is, in fact, the commencement of a great historical chant, similar in character to the 78th Psalm, or to some passages of the

Prophets, which in style it greatly resembles. In singing this portion, as also in the following litany to the chiefs, the long-drawn exclamation of hai, or haihhaih, is frequently introduced. In the MS. book referred to in the last note, the list of councillors was preceded by a paragraph, written like prose, but with many of these interjections interspersed through it. The interpreter, Albert Cusick, an intelligent and educated man, assured me that this was a song, and at my request he chanted a few staves of it, after the native fashion. The following are the words of this hymn, arranged as they are sung. It will be seen that it is a sort of cento or compilation, in the Onondaga dialect, of passages from various portions of the Canienga Book of Rites, and chiefly from the section (29) now under consideration:--

Haihhaih	Woe! Woe!
Jiyathontek	Hearken ye!
Niyonkha!	We are diminished!
Haihhaih	Woe! Woe!
Tejoskawayenton.	The cleared land has become a thicket.
Haihhaih!	
Skahentahenyon.	Woe! Woe!
Hai!	The clear places are deserted.
Shatyherarta--	Woe!
Hotyiwisahongwe--	They are in their graves--
Hai!	They who established it--
Kayaneengoha.	Woe!
Netikenen honen	The great League.
Nene kenyoiwatatye--	Yet they declared
Kayaneengowane.	It should endure--
Hai!	The great League.
Wakaiwakayonnheha.	Woe!
Hai!	Their work has grown old.
Netho watyongwententhe.	Woe!
	Thus we are become miserable.

The closing word is the same as the Canienga watyonkwenendane, which is found in the closing section of the Canienga book. The lines of the Onondaga hymn which immediately precede this concluding word will be found in Section 20 of that book, a section which is probably meant to be chanted. It will be noticed that the lines of this hymn fall naturally into a sort of parallelism, like that of the Hebrew chants.

30. Dekarihaokenh, or Tehkarihhoken. In John Buck's MS. the list of chiefs is preceded by the words "Nene Tehadirihoken," meaning the Caniengas, or, literally, "the Tekarihokens." For an explanation of this idiom and name, see ante, p. 77. Ayonhwahtha, or Hayenwatha. This name, which, as Hiawatha, is now familiar to us as a household word, is rendered "He who seeks the wampum belt." Chief George Johnson thought it was derived from oyonwa, wampum-belt, and ratiehwatha, to look for something, or, rather, to seem to seek something which we know where to find. M. Cuoq refers the latter part of the word to the verb katha, to make. [1] The termination atha is, in this sense, of frequent occurrence in Iroquois compounds. The name would then mean "He who makes the wampum-belt," and would account for the story which ascribes to Hiawatha the invention of wampum. The Senecas, in whose language the word oyonwa has ceased to exist, have corrupted the name to Hayowentha, which they render "he who combs." This form of the name has also produced its legend, which is referred to elsewhere (p. 87). Hiawatha "combed the snakes out of Atotarho's head," when he brought that redoubted chief into the confederacy.

Shatekariwate, "two equal statements," or "two things equal." This name is derived from sate or shate, equal, and kariwa, or karihwa, for which see the Glossary.

Etho natejonhne, "this was your number," or, this was the extent of your class. These words, or the similar form, etho natehadinhne, "this was their number," indicate apparently that the roll of chiefs belonging to a particular class or clan is completed. They are followed by three other words which have been already explained (ante, pages 33 and 80), sewaterihwakhaonghkwe, sewarihwisaanonghkwe, kayanerenhkowa; In the written litany these three words are omitted toward the close,-- probably to save the penman the labor of transcription; but in the actual ceremony it is understood that they are chanted wherever the formula etho natejonhne, or etho natehadinhne, occurs. In the modern Canienga speech this verb is thus conjugated in the plural,--etho being contracted to eh.—

---

[1] Lexique de la Langue Iroquois, p. 161.

ehnatetioñhne,	we were that number;
ehnatejioñhne,	ye were that number;
ehnatehadiñhne,	they were that number.

The three Canienga councillors of the first class all belong to the Tortoise clan.

31. Sharenhowane; in Onondaga, Showenhona. This name was translated by the interpreters, "he is the loftiest tree." It seems properly to mean "he is a great tree-top," from karenha, or garenha, which Bruyas renders cime d'arbre, and kowane, great.

Deyonnhehgonh, or Teyonhehkwen, "double life," from onnhe, life. My friend, Chief George Johnson, who bears this titular appellation, tells me that it is property the name of a certain shrub, which has a great tenacity of life.

Ohrenregowah; in Onondaga, Owenhegona. The interpreters differed much in opinion as to the meaning of this name. Some said "wide branches;" another, "a high hill." The root-word, ohrenre, is obsolete, and its meaning is apparently lost.

The three chiefs of the second class or division of the Caniengas belong to the Wolf clan.

32. Dehennakarine; in Onondaga, Tehennakaihne; "going with two horns." The root is onakara, horn, the termination ine, or ihne, gives the sense of going, de or te is the duplicative prefix.

Aghstawenserontha (Onon. Hastawensenwa), "he puts on the rattles." Mr. Bearfoot writes, "Ohstawensera seems to have been a general name for anything denuded of flesh, but is now confined to the rattles of the rattlesnake."

Shosgoharowane (Onon. Shosgohaehna), "he is a great wood-drift." "Yohskoharo, (writes Mr. Bearfoot) means an obstruction by driftwood in creeks or small rivers. The councillors of the third Canienga class are of the Bear clan.

33. Ise seniyatagweniyohkwe, "ye two were the principals." Atagweniyo, or adakweniyu (see ante, note to Sec. 28) here becomes a verb in the imperfect tense and the dual number. The reference is either to Dekanawidah and Odatsehte, the chiefs of the Caniengas and Oneidas, who worked together in founding the confederacy, or, rather, perhaps, to their two nations, each regarded as an individual, and, in a manner, personified.

Jatatawhak, or, more properly jatatahwak, means, liter ally, "son of each other." It is from the root-word kahawak (or gahawak), which is defined by Bruyas, avoir pour enfant, and is in the reciprocal form. Here, however, it is understood to mean "father and son," in reference to the political relationship between the Canienga and Oneida nations.

Odatsehte (Onon., Tatshehte), "bearing a quiver,"--or the pouch in which the arrows are carried. According to the tradition, when Dekanawidah's brother and embassador formally adopted Odatsehte as the political son of the Canienga chief, he took the quiver off his own shoulder, and hung it upon that of the Oneida chieftain.

Kanonhgwenyodon, "setting up ears of corn in a row." From ononhkwenha, an ear of corn.

Deyohhagwente (Onon., Tyohagwente), "open voice" This is another obsolete, or semi-obsolete word, about which the interpreters differ widely in opinion. "Hollow tube," "windpipe," "opening in the woods," "open voice," were the various renderings suggested. The latter would be de rived from ohakwa or ohagwa, voice, and the termination wente or gwente, which gives the sense of "open."

The three chiefs of the first Oneida class belong to the Wolf clan.

34. Shononhsese (Onon., Shononses), "his long house," or, "he has a long house." From kanonsa, house, with the adjective termination es, long.

Daonahrokenagh (Onon., Tonaohgena), "two branches." This is another doubtful word. In modern Canienga, "two branches" would be Toneñrokeñ.

Atyatonentha (Onon., Hatyatonnentha), "he lowers himself," or, literally, "he slides himself down," from oyata, body, self, and tonnenta, to slide.

The councillors of the second Oneida class are of the Tortoise clan.

35. Dewatahonhtenyonk (Onon., Tehatahonhtenyonk), "two hanging ears," from ohonta, ear.

Kaniyatahshayonk (Onon., Kanenyatakshayen). This name was rendered "easy throat," as if derived from oniata, throat but the Oneida form of the word seems to point to a derivation from onenya (or onenhia), stone. This word must be regarded as another obsolete compound.

Onwatsatonhonk (Onon., Onwasjatenwi), "he is buried." The three chiefs of the third Oneida class are of the Bear clan.

36. Eghyesaotonnihsen, lit., "this was his uncle,"--or, as the words would be understood by the hearers, "the next are his uncles." The Onondaga nation, being the brother of the Canienga, was, of course, the uncle of the Oneida. In John Buck's MS. the Onondagas are introduced with more ceremony in the following lines:

Etho yeshodonnih;	These are the uncles;
Rodihsennakeghde,	They, the name-bearers
Tehhotiyena,	They took hold here;
Rodihnonsyonnihton.	They made the League.

That is, they helped, or joined, in making the League.

Thatotarho, Wathatotarho (Onon. Thatotarho). Thatotarho is the passive voice and cislocative form of otarho, which is defined "to grasp," or "catch" (accrocher), but in the passive signifies "entangled." This great chief. whose name is better known as Atotarho (without the cislocative prefix), is of the Bear clan.

Etho ronarasehsen, "these were cousins," or rather, "the next were cousins." This cousinhood, like all the relation ships throughout the book, is political, and indicates some close relationship in public affairs. The announcement applies to the following chiefs, Enneserarenh and Dehatkahthos, who were the special aids and counsellors of Atotarho.

The Iroquois Book of Rites

Enneserarenh (Onon. Hanesehen). One Onondaga chief said that he knew no meaning for this word. Another thought it might mean "the best soil uppermost." It is apparently from some obsolete root.

Dehatkahthos (Onon. Tehatkahtons), "he is two-sighted," or, "he looks both ways." Another rendering made it "on the watch." This and the preceding chief belong now to the Beaver clan. In one of the Onondaga lists which I received, these two, with their principal, Atotarho, formed a "class" by themselves, and were doubtless originally of the same clan.

Waghontenhnonterontye, "they were as brothers thenceforth;" or, more fully rendered, "the next continued to be brothers."

This declaration refers to the three next following chiefs, who were connected by some special political tie. The first who bore the name were, probably, like the two preceding chiefs, leading partisans and favorites of the first Atotarho.

Onyatajiwak, or Skanyadajiwak (Onon., Oyatajiwak). One authority makes this "a fowl's crop;" another, "the throat alone," from oniata, throat, and jiwak, alone; another defined it, "bitter threat." Mr. Morgan renders it "bitter body,"--his informant probably seeing in it the word oyata, body. This chief belongs now to the Snipe clan.

Awekeyade, "the end of its journey,"--from awe, going, and akonhiate (Can.) "at the end." This chief is of the Ball tribe, both in Canada and at Onondaga Castle. In the list furnished to Mr. Morgan by the Senecas, he is of the Tortoise clan.

Dehadkwarayen (Onon., Tehatkwayen). This word is obsolete. One interpreter guessed it to mean "on his body;" another made it "red wings." He is of the Tortoise clan. In the Book of Rites the first six chiefs of the Onondagas make but one class, as is shown by the fact that their names are followed by the formula, etho natejonhne, "this was the number of you." It may be presumed that they were originally of one clan,--probably that of the Bear, to which their leader, Atotarho, belonged.

37. Yeshohawak, rokwahhokowah, "then his next son, he the great Wolf." The chief who follows, Rononghwireghtonh, was evidently a personage of great importance,--probably the leading chief of the wolf class. He forms a

"clan" by himself,--the only instance of the kind in the list. The expression, "there (or, in him) were combined the minds," indicates--as Mr. Bearfoot suggests--a superior intellect. It may also refer to the fact that he was the hereditary keeper of the wampum records. The title was borne in Canada by the late chief George Buck, but the duties of record-keeper were usually performed by his more eminent brother, John (Skanawati).

Rononghwireghtonh (Onon., Hononwiehti), "he is sunk out of sight." This chief, who, as has been stated, alone constitutes the second Onondaga class, is of the Wolf clan.

38. Etho yeshotonnyh tekadarakehne, "then his uncles of the two clans." The five chiefs, who follow probably bore sonic peculiar political relation to Rononghwireghton.

The first two in modern times are of the Deer clan; the last three are of the Eel clan. It is probable that they all belonged originally, with him, to one clan, that of the Wolf, and consequently to one class, which was afterwards divided into three.

Kawenenseronton (Onon., Kawenensenton). A word of doubtful meaning; one interpreter thought it meant "her voice suspended."

Haghriron (Onon., Hahihon), "spilled," or "scattered."

39. Wahhondennonterontye. This word has already occurred, with a different orthography, and is explained in the Note to Section 36.

Ronyennyennih (Onon., Honyennyenni). No satisfactory explanation could be obtained of this word. Chief john Buck did not know its meaning.

Shodakwarashonh (Onon., Shotegwashen), "he is bruised."

Shakokenghne (Onon. Shahkohkenneh), "he saw them." As stated above, the three chiefs in this class are of the Eel clan.

40. Shihonadewiraratye, "they had children," or, rather, "they continued to get children." Mr. Bearfoot writes in regard to this word: "Yodewirare, a fowl hatching, referring to the time when they were forming the league, when they were said to be hatching, or producing, the children mentioned--i.e., the other tribes who were taken into the confederacy."

Tehhodidarakeh, "these the two clans." Taken in connection with the preceding lines of the chant, it seems probable that this expression refers to the introduction of other clans into the Council besides the original three, the Bear, Wolf and Tortoise, which existed when the confederacy was formed.

Raserhaghrhonh (Onon., Sherhahwi), "wearing a hatchet in his belt," from asera, hatchet. This chief is of the Tortoise clan.

Etho wahhoronghyaronnyon, this put away the clouds. "These "clouds," it is said, were the clouds of war, which were dispelled by the great chief whose name is thus introduced, Skanawadyh, or as now spelt, Skanawati. He had the peculiar distinction of holding two offices, which were rarely combined. He was both a high chief, or "Lord of the Council," and a "Great Warrior." In former times the members of the Great Council seldom assumed executive duties. They were rarely sent out as ambassadors or is leaders of war-parties.

These duties were usually entrusted to the ablest chiefs of the second rank, who were known as "Great Warriors," rohskenrakehte-kowa. Skanawati was an exception to this rule. It would seem that the chief who first bore this title had special aptitudes, which have come down in his family. A striking in stance, given in the "Relations" of the Jesuit missionaries among the Hurons, has been admirably reproduced by Mr. Parkman in the twenty-third chapter of his "Jesuits in North America," and cannot be better told than in his words. In the year 1648, during the desperate war between the Kanonsionni and the Hurons, the Onondagas determined to respond to the pacific overtures which they had received from their northern foes.

"They chose for their envoy," continues the historian, Scandawati, a man of renown, sixty years of age, joining with him two colleagues.[1] The old Onondaga entered on his mission with a troubled mind. His anxiety was not so much for his life as for his honor and dignity; for, while the Oneidas and the Cayugas were acting in concurrence with the Onondagas, the Senecas

---

[1] Scandawati is the Huron--and probably the original Onondaga pronunciation of the name.

had refused any part in the embassy, and still breathed nothing but war. Would they, or still more, the Mohawks, so far forget the consideration due to one whose name had been great in the Councils of the League, as to assault the Hurons while he was among them in the character of an ambassador of his nation, whereby his honor would be compromised and his life endangered? 'I am not a dead dog,' he said, 'to be despised and forgotten. I am worthy that all men should turn their eyes on me while I am among enemies, and do nothing that may involve me in danger.' * * * Soon there came dire tidings. The prophetic heart of the old chief had not deceived him. The Senecas and Mohawks, disregarding negotiations in which they had no part, and resolved to bring them to an end, were invading the country in force. It might be thought that the Hurons would take their revenge on the Onondaga envoys, now hostages among them; but they did not do so, for the character of an ambassador was, for the most part, held in respect. One morning, however, Scandawati had disappeared. They were full of excitement; for they thought that he had escaped to the enemy. They ranged the woods in search of him, and at length found him in a thicket near the town. He lay dead, on a bed of spruce boughs which he had made, his throat deeply gashed with a knife. He had died by his own hand, a victim of mortified pride. 'See,' writes Father Ragueneau, 'how much our Indians stand on the point of honor!'"

It is worthy of note that the same aptitude for affairs and the same keen sense of honor which distinguished this high spirited chief survives in the member of his family who, on the Canadian Reservation, now bears the same title,--Chief John Buck,--whom his white neighbors all admit to be both a capable ruler and an able and trustworthy negotiator.

In Canada Skanawati is of the Tortoise clan. At Onondaga, where the original family has probably died out, the title now belongs to the Ball clan.

41. Yeshohawak, "then his next son,"--or rather, perhaps, "then, next, his son." The Cayuga nation was politically the son of the Onondaga nation.

Tekahenyonk (Onon., Hakaenyonk), "he looks both ways," or, "he examines warily." In section 28 (ante p. 126) this name is spelt Akahenyonh. The prefixed te is the duplicative particle, and gives the meaning of "spying on both sides." This and the following chief belong, in Canada, to the Deer clan, and constitute the first Cayuga class.

Jinontaweraon (Onon., Jinontaweyon), "coming on its knees."

42. Katakwarasonh (Onon., Katagwajik), "it was bruised." This name, it will be seen, is very similar to that of an Onondaga chief,--ante, Note to Section 39. The chief now named and the one who follows are of the Bear clan.

Shoyonwese (Onon., Soyonwes), "he has a long wampum belt." The root-word of this name is oyonwa, wampum-belt, the same that appears in Hayonwatha.

Atyaseronne (Onon., Hatyasenne), "he puts one on an other," or "he piles on." This chief is of the Tortoise clan, and completes, with the two preceding councillors, the second Cayuga class.

43. Yeshonadadekenah, "then they who are brothers." The three chiefs who follow are all of the Wolf clan, and make the third class of the Cayuga councillors.

Teyoronghyonkeh (Onon., Thowenyongo), "it touches the sky."

Teyodhoreghkonh (Onon., Tyotowegwi), "doubly cold."

Wathyawenhehetken (Onon., Thaowethon), "mossy place."

44. The two following chiefs are of the Snipe clan, and constitute the fourth and last Cayuga class.

Atontaraheha (Onon., Hatontaheha) "crowding himself in."

Teskahe (Onon., Heskahe) "resting on it."

45. Yeshotonnih, "and then his uncle." The Seneca nation, being the brother of the Onondaga, is, of course, the uncle of the Cayuga nation.

Skanyadariyo (Onon., Kanyataio), "beautiful lake; originally, perhaps, "great lake." (See Appendix, Note B.) This name is spelt in Section 28 (ante, p. 128) Kanyadariyu. The prefixed s is the sign of the reiterative form, and when joined to proper names is regarded as a token of nobility, like the French de, or the German von [1]. Kanyadariyo, was one of the two leading chiefs of the Senecas at the formation of the confederacy. The title belongs to the Wolf clan.

Yeshonaraseshen, lit., "they were cousins." In the present instance, and according to the Indian idiom, we must read "Skanyadariyo, with his cousin, Shadekaronyes."

Shadekaronyes (Onon., Shatekaenyes), "skies of equal length." This chief (whose successor now belongs to the Snipe clan) was in ancient times the head of the second great division of the Senecas.

These two potentates were made a "class" in the Council by themselves, and were thus required to deliberate together and come to an agreement on any question that was brought up, before expressing an opinion in the council. This ingenious device for preventing differences between the two sections of the Seneca nation is one of the many evidences of statesman ship exhibited in the formation of the League.

46. Satyenawat, "withheld." This chief, in the Canadian list, is of the Snipe clan; in Mr. Morgan's Seneca list, he is of the Bear clan. His comrade in the class, Shakenjowane, is, in both lists, of the Hawk clan.

Shakenjowane (Onon., Shakenjona), "large forehead."

There has apparently been some derangement here in the order of the classes. In Mr. Morgan's list, and also in one furnished to me at Onondaga Castle, the two chiefs just named belong to different classes. The variance of the lists may be thus shown:--

The Book of Rites.	The Seneca and Onondaga Lists.
Second Seneca Class.	
Satyenawat	Kanokarih
Shakenjowane	Shakenjowane.

---

[1] See J. A. Cuoq: Jugement Erroné, etc., p. 57, "Le reiteratif est comme un signe de noblesse dans les noms propres."

Third Seneca Class.

Kanokarih	Satyenawat
Nisharyenen	Nisharyenen.

Satyenawat and Kanokarih have changed places. As the Book of Rites is the earlier authority, it is probable that the change was made among the New York Senecas after a part of their nation had removed to Canada.

47. Kanokarih (Onon., Kanokaehe), "threatened."

Nisharyenen (Onon., Onishayenenha), "the day fell down."

One of the interpreters rendered the latter name, "the handle drops." The meaning of the word must be considered doubtful. The first of these chiefs is of the Tortoise clan, and the second is, in Canada, of the Bear clan. In Mr. Morgan's list he is of the Snipe clan. The disruption of the Seneca nation, and the introduction of Dew clans, have thrown this part of the list into confusion.

48. Onghwakeghaghshonah, etc. The verses which follow are repeated here from the passage of the Book which precedes the chanted litany. (See ante, Sect I on 28.) Their repetition is intended to introduce the names of the two chiefs who composed the fourth and last class of the Seneca councillors.

Yatehhotihohhataghkwen, "they were at the doorway," or, according to another version, "they made the doorway." The chiefs are represented as keeping the doorway of the "extended mansion," which imaged the confederacy.

Kanonghkeridawyh, (Onon., Kanonkeitawi,) "entangled hair given." This chief, in Canada, is of the Bear clan; in New York, according to Morgan's list, he is of the Snipe clan.

Teyoninhokarawenh, (Onon., Teyoninhokawenh,) "open door." In both lists he is of the Wolf clan.

Mr. Morgan (in his "League of the Iroquois," page 68,) states that to the last-named chief, or "sachem," the duty of watching the door was assigned, and that "they gave him a sub-sachem, or assistant, to enable him to execute this trust." In fact, however, every high chief, or royaner (lord), had an assistant, or war chief (roskenrakehte-kowa, great warrior), to execute his instructions. The Book of Rites shows clearly that the two chiefs to whom the duty of "guarding the door way" was assigned were both nobles of the first rank. Their office also appears not to have been warlike. From the words of the Book it would seem that when new tribes were received into the confederacy, these two councillors had the formal office of "opening the doorway" to the new-comers--that is (as we may suppose), of receiving and introducing their chiefs into the federal council.

In another sense the whole Seneca nation was deemed, and was styled in council, the Doorkeeper (Ronhohonti, pl.,--Roninhohonti) of the confederacy. The duty of guarding the common country against the invasions of the hostile tribes of the west was specially committed to them. Their leaders, or public representatives, in this duty would naturally be the two great chiefs of the nation, Kanyateriyo and Shadekaronyes. The rules of the League, however, seem to have for bidden the actual assumption by the councillors of any executive or warlike command. At least, if they undertook such duties, it must be as private men, and not in their capacity of nobles--just as an English peer might serve as an officer in the army or as an embassador. The only exceptions recognized by the Iroquois constitution seem to have been in the cases of Tekarihoken and Skanawati, who were at once nobles and war-chiefs. (See ante, pages 78 and 159.) The two great Seneca chiefs would therefore find it necessary to make over their military functions to their assistants or war-chiefs. This may explain the statement made by Morgan ("League of the Iroquois," p. 74) that there were two special "war-chiefships" created among the Senecas, to which these commands were assigned.

49. Onenh watyonkwentendane kanikonrakeh. The condoling chant concludes abruptly with the doleful exclamation, "Now we are dejected in spirit." Enkitendane, "I am becoming poor," or "wretched," is apparently a derivative of kitenre, to pity, and might be rendered, "I am in a pitiable state." "We are miserable in mind," would probably be a literal version of this closing ejaculation. Whether it is a lament for the past glories of the confederacy, or for the chief who is mourned, is a question which those who sing the words at the present day would probably have a difficulty in answering. It is likely, however, that the latter cause of grief was in the minds of those who first composed the chant.

It is an interesting fact, as showing the antiquity of the names of the chiefs in the foregoing list, that at least a fourth of them are of doubtful etymology. That their meaning was well understood when they were borne by the founders of the League cannot be questioned. The changes of language or the uncertainties of oral transmission, in the lapse of four centuries, have made this large proportion of them either obsolete or so corrupt as to be no longer intelligible. Of all the names it may probably be affirmed with truth that the Indians who hear them recited think of their primitive meaning as little as we ourselves think of the meaning of the family names or the English titles of nobility which we hear or read. To the Iroquois of the present day the hereditary titles of their councillors are to use their own expression--"just names," and nothing more. It must not be supposed, however, that the language itself has altered in the same degree. Proper names, as is well known, when they become mere appellatives, discharged of significance, are much more likely to vary than the words of ordinary speech.

NOTES ON THE ONONDAGA BOOK

1 a. Yo o-nen o-nen wen ni sr te, "oh now--now this day." It will be noticed that this address of the "younger brothers" commences in nearly the same words which begin the speeches of the Canienga book. This similarity of language exists in other parts of the two books, though disguised by the difference of dialect, and also by the very irregular and corrupt spelling of the Onondaga book. To give some idea of this irregularity, and of the manner in which the words of this book are to be pronounced, several of these words are sub joined, with the pronunciation of the interpreter, represented in the orthography of the Canienga book:

Words as written.	As pronounced by La Fori.
wen ni sr te	wennisaate
ho gar a nyat	hogaenyat
son tar yen	sontahien
na ya ne	nayeneh
o shon ta gon gonar	osontagongona
gar weear har tye	gawehehatie
on gwr non sen shen tar qua	ongwanonsenshentakwa
ga nen ar ta (or, ga nen ar ti)	ganenhate
kon hon wi sats	konthonwitsas
o wen gr ge	ohwengage
nar ya he yr genh	nayehiyaken.

The letter r, it will be seen, is not a consonant. In fact, it is never heard as such in the modern Onondaga dialect. As used by La Fort, its office is either to give to the preceding vowel a the sound which it has in father, or by itself to represent that sound. The a, when not followed by r, is usually sounded like a in fate, but sometimes keeps the sound of a in far. The e usually represents the English e in be, or, when followed by n, the e in pen. The i and y are commonly sounded as in the word city. The g is always hard, and is interchangeable with k. The t and d are also interchangeable.

While the syllables in the original are written separately, the words are not always distinguished; and it is doubtful if, in printing, they have in all cases been properly divided. The translation of the interpreter, though tolerably exact, was not always literal; and in the brief time at our command the precise meaning of some of the words was not ascertained. No attempt, therefore, has been made to form a glossary of this portion of the text.

(Transcribers' Note: In the original printed text there were gaps of one and two spaces between syllables. In this transcription the gaps of one space have been replaced with a hyphen and gaps of two spaces by one space.-- jbh.}

In the original the addresses of the "younger brothers" are divided into sections, which are numbered from one to seven, and each of which, in the ceremony, is called to mind by its special wampum-string, which is produced when the section is recited. As the first of these sections is of much greater length than the others, it has been divided in this work, for the purpose of ready reference, into sub-sections, which are numbered 1 a, 1 b, and so on.

1. b. Nenthaotagenhetak, "by the ashes," or "near the hearth." The root-word is here agenhe, the Onondaga form of the Canienga word akenra, ashes, which is comprised in the compound form, jiudakenrokde, in Section 27 of the Canienga book. It will be seen that the spokesman of the younger nations is here complying strictly with the law laid down in that section. He "stands by the hearth and speaks a few words to comfort those who are mourning."

1. c. "It was valued at twenty." The interpreters explained that by "twenty" was understood the whole of their wampum, which constituted all their treasure. A human life was worth the whole of this, and they freely gave it, merely to recall the memory of the chief who was gone. Among the Hurons, when a man had been killed, and his kindred were willing to renounce their claim to vengeance on receiving due satisfaction, the number of presents of wampum and other valuables which were to be given was rigidly prescribed by their customary law. [1] From this custom would easily follow the usage of making similar gifts, in token of sympathy, to all persons who were mourning the loss of a near relative.

---

[1] Relation of 1648, p. 80.

1. d. "Because with her the line is lost." The same sentiment prevailed among the Hurons. "For a Huron killed by a Huron," writes Father Ragueneau in the letter just quoted, "thirty gifts are commonly deemed a sufficient satisfaction. For a woman forty are required, because, as they say, the women are less able to defend themselves; and, moreover, they being the source whence the land is peopled, their lives should be deemed of more value to the commonwealth, and their weakness should have a stronger support in public justice." Such was the reasoning of these heathen barbarians. Enlightened Christendom has hardly yet advanced to the mark of these opinions.

1. e. "Where the grave has been made," &c. The recital of Father Ragueneau also illustrates this passage." Then followed," he writes, "nine other presents, for the purpose, as it were, of erecting a sepulchre for the deceased. Four of them were for the four pillars which should support this sepulchre, and four others for the four cross-pieces on which the bier of the dead was to rest. The ninth was to serve as his pillow."

2. "I will make the sky clear to you." In this paragraph the speaker reminds the mourners, in the style of bold imagery which the Iroquois orators affected, that continued grief for the dead would not be consonant with the course of nature. Though all might seem dark to them now, the sky would be as clear, and the sun would shine as brightly for them, as if their friend had not died. Their loss had been inevitable, and equally sure would be the return of the "pleasant days." This reminder, which may seem to us needless, was evidently designed as a reproof, at once gentle and forcible, of those customs of excessive and protracted mourning which were anciently common among the Huron Iroquois tribes.

3. "You must converse with your nephews," &c. The "nephews" are, of course, the chiefs of the younger nations, who are here the condolers. The mourners are urged to seek for comfort in the sympathy of their friends, and not to reject the consolations offered by their visitors and by their own people.

4. "And now you can go out before the people, and go on with your duties," &c. This, it will be seen, corresponds with the injunctions of the Canienga book. (See Section 27, ante, p. 127): "And then they will be comforted, and will conform to the great law."

The Iroquois Book of Rites

6. "Then the horns shall be left on the grave," &c. The same figure is here used as in the Canienga book, Section 23 (ante, p. 125). It is evident that the importance of keeping up the succession of their councillors was constantly impressed on the minds of the Iroquois people by the founders of their League.

7. "And the next death will receive the pouch." The "mourning wampum," in modern days, is left, or supposed to be left, with the kindred of the late chief until another death shall occur among the members of the Council, when it is to be passed on to the family of the deceased. This economy is made necessary by the fact that only one store of such wampum now exists, as the article is no longer made. It is probable that in ancient times the wampum was left permanently with the family of the deceased, as a memorial of the departed chief.

"Where the fire is made and the smoke is rising," i.e., when you receive notice that a Condoling Council is to be held in a certain place. The kindled fire and the rising smoke were the well-understood images which represented the convocation of their councils. In the Onondaga book before referred to (ante, p. 152) a few pages were occupied by what might be styled a pagan sermon, composed of exhortations addressed to the chiefs, urging them to do their duty to the community. The following is the commencement of this curious composition, which may serve to illustrate both the words now under consideration and the character of the people. The orthography is much better than that of La Fort's book, the vowels generally having the Italian sound, and the spelling being tolerably uniform. The translation was made by Albert Cusick, and is for the most part closely literal. The discourse commences with a "text," after the fashion which the pagan exhorter had probably learned from the missionaries:--

Naye ne iwaton ne gayanencher:

Onen wahagwatatjistagenhas ne Thatontarho. Onen wagayengwaeten, naye ne watkaenya, esta netho tina enyontkawaonk. Ne enagenyon nwatkaonwenjage shanonwe nwakayengwaeten netho titentyetongenta shanonwe nwakayengwaeten, ne tokat gishens enyagoiwayentaha ne oyatonwetti.

Netho hiya nigawennonten ne ongwanencher ne Ayakt Niyongyonwenjage ne Tyongwehonwe.

Otti nawahoten ne oyengwaetakwit? Nayehiya, ne agwegeh enhonatiwagwaisyonk ne hatigowanes,--tenhontatnonongwak gagweki,--oni enshagotino-ongwak ne honityogwa; engenk ne hotisgenrhergeta, oni ne genthonwisash, oni ne hongwagsata, oni ne ashonsthateyetigaher ne ongwagsata; netho niyoh tehatinya agweke sne sgennon enyonnontonnyonhet,ne hegentyogwagwegi. Naye ne hatigowanens neye gagwegi honatiiwayenni sha oni nenyotik honityogwa shanya yagonigonheten. Ne tokat gishen naye enyagotiwatentyeti, negaewane akwashen ne honiyatwa shanityawenih.

Translation.

"The law says this:"

"Now the council-fire was lighted by Atotarho. Now the smoke rises and ascends to the sky, that everybody may see it. The tribes of the different nations where the smoke appeared shall come directly where the smoke arises, if, perhaps, they have any business for the council to consider.

"These are the words of our law,--of the Six Nations of Indians.

"What is the purpose of the smoke? It is this--that the chiefs must all be honest; that they must all love one another; and that they must have regard for their people,--including the women, and also our children, and also those children whom we have not yet seen; so much they must care for, that all may be in peace, even the whole nation. It is the duty of the chiefs to do this, and they have the power to govern their people. If there is anything to be done for the good of the people, it is their duty to do it."

7 b. "Now I have finished! Now show him to me!" With this laconic exclamation, which calls upon the nation of the late chief to bring forward his successor, the formal portion of the ceremony--the condolence which precedes the installation--is abruptly closed.

APPENDIX

THE NAMES OF THE IROQUOIS NATIONS

THE meaning of the term Kanonsionni, and of the other names by which the several nations were known in their Council, are fully explained in the Introduction. But some account should be given of the names, often inappropriate and generally much corrupted, by which they were known to their white neighbors. The origin and proper meaning of the word Iroquois are doubtful. All that can be said with certainty is that the explanation given by Charlevoix cannot possibly be correct. "The name of Iroquois," he says, "is purely French, and has been formed from the term hiro, 'I have spoken,' a word by which these Indians close all their speeches, and koué, which, when long drawn out, is a cry of sorrow, and when briefly uttered, is an exclamation of joy."[1] It might be enough to say of this derivation that no other nation or tribe of which we have any knowledge has ever borne a name composed in this whimsical fashion. But what is decisive is the fact that Champlain had learned the name from his Indian allies before he or any other Frenchman, so far as is known, had ever seen an Iroquois. It is probable that the origin of the word is to be sought in the Huron language; yet, as this is similar to the Iroquois tongue, an attempt may be made to find a solution in the latter. According to Bruyas, the word garokwa meant a pipe, and also a piece of tobacco,--and, in its verbal form, to smoke. This word is found, somewhat disguised by aspirates, in the Book of Rites, denighroghkwayen,---let us two smoke together." (Ante, p. 115, Section 2). In the indeterminate form the verb becomes ierokwa, which is certainly very near to "Iroquois." It might be rendered "they who smoke," or "they who use tobacco," or, briefly, "the Tobacco People." This name, the Tobacco Nation (Nation du Petun) was given by the French, and probably also by the Algonkins, to one of the Huron tribes, the Tionontates, noted for the excellent tobacco which they raised and sold. The Iroquois were equally well known for their cultivation of this plant, of which they had a choice variety.[2] It is possible that their northern neighbors may have given to them also a name derived from this industry. Another not

---

[1] History of New France, Vol. i, p. 270.
[2] "The Senecas still cultivate tobacco. Its name signifies 'the only tobacco,' because they consider this variety superior to all others."--Morgan: League of the Iroquois, p. 375.

improbable supposition might connect the name with that of a leading sept among them, the Bear clan. This clan, at least among the Caniengas, seems to have been better known than any other to their neighbors. The Algonkins knew that nation as the Maquas, or Bears. In the Canienga speech, bear is ohkwai,--in Onondaga, the word becomes ohkwai, and in Cayuga, iakwai,--which also is not far from Iroquois. These conjectures--for they are nothing more--may both be wrong; but they will perhaps serve to show the direction in which the explanation of this perplexing word is to be sought.

The name of Mingo or Mengwe, by which the Iroquois were known to the Delawares and the other southern Algonkins, is said to be a contraction of the Lenape word Mahongwi, meaning the "People of the Springs."[1] The Iroquois possessed the headwaters of the rivers which flowed through the country of the Delawares,--and this explanation of the name may therefore be accepted as a probable one.

The first of the Iroquois nations, the "oldest brother" of the confederacy, has been singularly unfortunate in the designations by which it has become generally known. The people have a fine, sonorous name of their own, said to be derived from that of one of their ancient towns. This name is Kanienke, "at the Flint." Kanien, in their language, signifies flint, and the final syllable is the same locative particle which we find in Onontake, "at the mountain." In pronunciation and spelling, this, like other Indian words, is much varied, both by the natives themselves and by their white neighbors, becoming Kanieke, Kanyenke, Canyangeh, and Canienga. The latter form, which accords with the sister names of Onondaga and Cayuga, has been adopted in the present volume.

The Huron frequently drops the initial k, or changes it to y. The Canienga people are styled in that speech Yanyenge, a word which is evidently the origin of the name of Agnier, by which this nation is known to the French.

The Dutch learned from the Mohicans (whose name, signifying Wolves, is supposed to be derived from that of their leading clan) to call the Kanienke by the corresponding name of Maqua (or Makwa), the Algonkin word for Bear. But as the Iroquois, and especially the Caniengas, became more and more a terror to the surrounding nations, the feelings of aversion and

---

[1] E. G. Squier: "Traditions of the Algonquins," in Beach's Indian Miscellany, p. 28.

dread thus awakened found vent in an opprobrious epithet, which the southern and eastern Algonkins applied to their obnoxious neighbors. They were styled by these enemies Mowak, or Mowawak, a word which has been corrupted to Mohawk. It is the third person plural, in the sixth "transition," of the Algonkin word mowa, which means "to eat," but which is only used of food that has had life. Literally it means "they eat them;" but the force of the verb and of the pronominal inflection suffices to give to the word, when used as an appellative, the meaning of "those who eat men," or, in other words, "the Cannibals." That the English, with whom the Caniengas were always fast friends, should have adopted this uncouth and spiteful nickname is somewhat surprising. It is time that science and history should combine to banish it, and to resume the correct designation. [1]

The name Oneida, which in French became Onneyouth or Onneyote, is a corruption of a compound word, formed of onenhia, or onenya, stone, and kaniote, to be upright or elevated. Onenniote is rendered "the projecting stone." It is applied to a large boulder of syennite, which thrusts its broad shoulder above the earth at the summit of an eminence near which, in early times, the Oneidas had planted their chief settlement.

As has been already stated, Onondaga is a softened pronunciation of Onontake, "at the mountain,"--or, perhaps, more exactly, "at the hill." It is probable that this name was unknown when the confederacy was formed, as it is not comprised in the list of towns given in the Book of Rites. It may be supposed to have been first applied to this nation after their chief town was removed to the site which it occupied in the year 1654, when the first white visitors of whom we have any certain account, the Jesuit Father Le Moyne and his party, came among them,--and also in 1677, when the English explorer, Greenhalgh, passed through their country. This site was about seven miles east of their present Reservation. I visited it in September, 1880, in company with my friend, General John S. Clark, who has been singularly successful in identifying the positions of the ancient Iroquois towns. The locality is thus described in my journal: "The site is, for an Indian town, peculiarly striking and attractive. It stretches about three

---

[1] William Penn and his colonists, who probably understood the meaning of the word Mohawk, forbore to employ it. In the early records of the colony (published by the Pennsylvania Historical Society) the nation is described in treaties, laws, and other public acts, by its proper designation, a little distorted in the spelling,-- Canyingoes, Ganyingoes, Cayinkers, etc.

miles in length, with a width of half a mile, along the broad back and gently sloping sides of a great hill, which swells, like a vast oblong cushion, between two hollows made by branches of a small stream, known as Limehouse creek. These streams and many springs on the hillside yielded abundance of water, while the encircling ridges on every side afforded both firewood and game. In the neighborhood were rich valleys, where--as well as on the hill itself--the people raised their crops of corn, beans, pumpkins, and tobacco. There are signs of a large population." In the fields of stubble which occupied the site of this ancient capital, the position of the houses could still be traced by the dark patches of soil; and a search of an hour or two rewarded us with several wampum-beads, flint chips, and a copper coin of the last century. The owner of the land, an intelligent farmer, affirmed that "wagon-loads" of Indian wares,--pottery, hatchets, stone implements, and the like-had been carried off by curiosity seekers.

The name of the Cayugas (in French Goyogouin) is variously pronounced by the Iroquois themselves. I wrote it as I heard it, at different times, from members of the various tribes, Koyu^{n}kweñ, Koiu^{n}kwe, Kwaiu^{n}kweñ, Kayu^{n}kwe. A Cayuga chief made it Kayu^{n}kwa, which is very near the usual English pronunciation of the word. Of its purport no satisfactory account could be obtained. One interpreter rendered it "the fruit country;--another "the place where canoes are drawn out." Cusick, the historian, translates it "a mountain rising from the water." Mr. Morgan was told that it meant "the mucky land." We can only infer that the interpreters were seeking, by vague resemblances, to recover a lost meaning.

The Senecas, who were called by the French Tsonontouan or Sonnontouan, bore among the Iroquois various names, but all apparently derived from the words which appear in that appellation,--ononta, hill, and kowa or kowane, great. The Caniengas called them Tsonontowane; the Oneidas abridged the word to Tsontowana; the Cayugas corrupted it to Onondewa; and the Onondagas contracted it yet farther, to Nontona. The Senecas called themselves variously Sonontowa, Onontewa, and Nondewa. Sonontowane is probably the most correct form.

The word Seneca is supposed to be of Algonkin origin, and, like Mohawk, to have been given as an expression of dislike, or rather of hostility. Sinako, in the Delaware tongue, means properly "Stone Snakes;" but in this conjunction it is understood, according to the interpretation furnished to Mr.

Squier, to signify "Mountain Snakes."[1] The Delawares, it appears, were accustomed to term all their enemies "snakes." In this case they simply translated the native name of the Iroquois tribe (the "Mountain People"), and added this uncomplimentary epithet. As the name, unlike the word Mohawk, is readily pronounced by the people to whom it was given, and as they seem to have in some measure accepted it, there is not the same reason for objecting to its use as exists in the case of the latter word,--more especially as there is no absolute certainty that it is not really an Iroquois word. It bears, in its present form, a close resemblance to the honorable "Council name" of the Onondagas,--Sennakehte, "the title-givers;" a fact which may perhaps have made the western nation more willing to adopt it.

---

[1] "Traditions of the Algonquins," in Beach's Indian Miscellany, p. 33.

MEANING OF OHIO, ONTARIO, ONONTIO, RAWENNIIO

THE words Ohio, Ontario and Onontio (or Yonnondio)-which should properly be pronounced as if written Oheeyo, Ontareeyo, and Ononteeyo--are commonly rendered "Beautiful River," "Beautiful Lake," "Beautiful Mountain." This, doubtless, is the meaning which each of the words conveys to an Iroquois of the present day, unless he belongs to the Tuscarora tribe. But there can be no doubt that the termination io (otherwise written iyo, iio, eeyo, etc.) had originally the sense, not of "beautiful," but of "great." It is derived from the word wiyo (or wiio) which signifies in the Seneca dialect good, but in the Tuscarora, great. It is certain that the Tuscaroras have preserved the primitive meaning of the word, which the Hurons and the proper Iroquois have lost. When the French missionaries first studied the languages of these nations, traces of the original usage were apparent. Bruyas, in the "Proemium" to his Radices Verborum Iroquæorum, (p. 14), expressly states that jo (io) in composition with verbs, "signifies magnitude." He gives as an example, garih8ioston, "to make much of anything," from garth8a, thing, and io, "great, important." The Jesuit missionaries, in their Relation for 1641, (p. 22) render Onontio "great mountain," and say that both Hurons and Iroquois gave this title to the Governor of that day as a translation of his name, Montmagny.

Ontario is derived from the Huron yontare, or ontare, lake (Iroquois, oniatare), with this termination. It was not by any means the most beautiful of the lakes which they knew; but in the early times, when the Hurons dwelt on the north and east of it and the Iroquois on the south, it was to both of them emphatically "the great lake."

Ohio, in like manner, is derived, as M. Cuoq in the valuable notes to his Lexicon (p. 159) informs us, from the obsolete ohia, river, now only used in the compound form ohionha. Ohia, coalescing with this ancient affix, would become ohiio, or ohiyo, with the signification of "great river," or, as the historian Cusick renders it, "principal stream."

M. Cuoq, in his "Etudes Philologiques" (p. 14) has well explained the interesting word Rawenniio, used in various dialectical forms by both Hurons and Iroquois, as the name of the deity. It signifies, as he informs us, "he is master," or, used as a noun, "he who is master." This, of course, is the modern acceptation; but we can gather from the ancient Huron grammar, translated by Mr. Wilkie, (ante, p. 101) that the word had once, as might be supposed, a larger meaning. The phrase," it is the great master," in that grammar (p. 108) is rendered ondaieaat etharontio or etha8endio. The Huron nd becomes in Iroquois nn. Etha8endio is undoubtedly a form of the same word which appears in the Iroquois Rawenniio. We thus learn that the latter word meant originally not merely "the master," but "the great master." Its root is probably to be found in the Iroquois kawen, or gawen (Bruyas, p. 64), which signifies "to belong to any one," and yields, in. combination with oyata, person, the derivatives gaiatawen, to have for subject, and gaiatawenston, to subject any one.

THE ERA OF THE CONFEDERACY

MR. Morgan, in his work on "Systems of Consanguinity and Affinity of the Human Family" (p. 151), fixes the date of the formation of the Iroquois league at about the middle of the fifteenth century. He says: "As near as can now be ascertained, the league had been established about one hundred and fifty years when Champlain, in 1609, first encountered the Mohawks within their own territories, on the west coast of Lake George. This would place the epoch of its formation about A. D., 1459." Mr. Morgan, as he informed me, deduced this conclusion from the testimony of the most intelligent Indians whom he had consulted on the subject. His informants belonged chiefly to the Seneca and Tuscarora nations. Their statements are entirely confirmed by those of the Onondaga record-keepers, both on the Syracuse Reservation and in Canada. When the chiefs at Onondaga Castle, who, in October, 1875, met to explain to me their wampum records, were asked how long it had been since their league was made, they replied (as I find the answer recorded in my notes) that "it was their belief that the confederacy was formed about six generations before the white people came to these parts." Hudson ascended the river to which he gave his name in September, 1609. A boat from his ship advanced beyond Albany, and consequently into the territories of the League. "Frequent intercourse," says Bancroft, in his account of this exploration, "was held with the astonished natives of the Algonquin race; and the strangers were welcomed by a deputation from the Mohawks." If we allow twenty-five years to a generation, the era of the confederacy is carried back to a period a hundred and fifty years before the date of Hudson's discovery,--or to the year 1459. This statement of the Onondaga chiefs harmonizes, therefore, closely with that which Mr. Morgan had heard among the other nations.

I afterwards (in 1882) put the same question to my friend, Chief John Buck, the keeper of the wampum-records of the Canadian Iroquois. He thought it was then "about four hundred years" since the League was formed. He was confident that it was before any white people had been heard of by his nation. This opinion accords sufficiently with the more definite statement of the New York Onondagas to be deemed a confirmation of that statement.

There are two authorities whose opinions differ widely, in opposite directions, from the information thus obtained by Mr. Morgan and myself. David Cusick, in his "Sketches of Ancient History of the Six Nations," supposes that the League was formed "perhaps 1000 years before Columbus discovered America." His reasons for this supposition, however, do not bear examination. He makes Atotarho the hereditary title of a monarch, like Pharaoh or Cæsar, and states that thirteen potentates bearing that title had "reigned" between the formation of the confederacy and the discovery of America by Columbus. The duration of each of these reigns he computes, absurdly enough, at exactly fifty years, which, however, would give altogether a term of only six hundred and fifty years. He supposes the discovery of America to have taken place during the reign of the thirteenth Atotarho; and he adds that the conquest and dispersion of the Eries occurred "about this time." The latter event, as we know, took place in 1656. It is evident that Cusick's chronology is totally at fault. As an Iroquois chief was never succeeded by his son, but often by his brother, it is by no means improbable that thirteen persons may have held successively the title of Atotarho in the term of nearly two centuries, between the years 1459 and 1656.

On the other hand, Heckewelder, in his well-known work on the "History, Manners and Customs of the Indian Nations," cites a passage from a manuscript book of his predecessor, the Rev. C. Pyrlæus, formerly missionary among the Mohawks, from which a comparatively recent date would be inferred for the confederation. The inference, however, is probably due to a mistake of Heckewelder himself. The passage, as it stands in his volume, [1] is as follows:--

"The Rev. C. Pyrlæus, in his manuscript book, p. 234, says: 'The alliance or confederacy of the Five Nations was established, as near as can be conjectured, one age (or the length of a man's life) before the white people (the Dutch) came into the country. Thannawage was the name of the aged Indian, a Mohawk, who first proposed such an alliance.'"

---

[1] p. 56 of the revised edition of 1875, published by the Historical Society of Pennsylvania.

The words which Heckewelder has here included between parentheses are apparently explanations which he himself added to the original statement of Pyrlæus. The first of these glosses, by which an "age" is explained to be the length of a man's life, is doubtless correct; but the second, which identifies the "white people" of Pyrlæus with the Dutch, is probably wrong. The white people who first "came into the country" of the Huron-Iroquois nations were the French, under Cartier. It was in the summer of 1535 that the bold Breton navigator, with three vessels commissioned to establish a colony in Canada, entered the St. Lawrence, and ascended the great river as far as the sites of Quebec and Montreal. He spent the subsequent winter at Quebec. The presence of this expedition, with its soldiers and sailors of strange complexion and armed with terrible weapons, must have been known to all the tribes dwelling along the river, and would naturally make an epoch in their chronology. Assuming the year 1535 as the time when the white people first "came into the country," and taking "the length of a man's life" at seventy-five years (or three generations) we should arrive at the year 1460 as the date of the formation of the Iroquois League. [1]

The brief period allowed by Heckewelder's version is on many accounts inadmissible. If, when the Dutch first came among the Iroquois, the confederacy had existed for only about eighty years, there must have been many persons then living who had personally known some of its founders. It is quite inconceivable that the cloud of mythological legends which has gathered around the names of these founders--of which Clark, in his "Onondaga," gives only the smaller portion--should have arisen in so short a term. Nor is it probable that in so brief a period as has elapsed since the date suggested by Heckewelder, a fourth part of the names of the fifty chiefs who formed the first council would have become unintelligible, or at least doubtful in meaning. Schoolcraft, who was inclined to defer to Heckewelder's authority on this point, did so with evident doubt and perplexity. "We cannot," he says, "without rejecting many positive traditions of the Iroquois themselves, refuse to concede a much earlier

---

[1] There is an evident difference between the expression used by my p. 180 Onondaga informants and that which is quoted by Heckewelder from Pyrlæus. The latter speaks of the time before the white people "came into the country;" the Onondagas referred to the time before they "came to these parts." The passage cited from Bancroft seems to indicate that the white men of Hudson's crew presented no novel or startling aspect to the Mohawks. The French had been "in the country" before them.

period to the first attempts of these interesting tribes to form a general political association." [1]

In view of all the facts there seems no reason for withholding credence from the clear and positive statement of the Iroquois chroniclers, who place the commencement of their confederate government at about the middle of the fifteenth century.

---

[1] "Notes on the Iroquois." p. 75.

THE HIAWATHA MYTHS

WHILE many of the narratives of preternatural events recounted by Clark, Schoolcraft and others, in which the name of Hiawatha occurs, are merely adaptations of older myths relating to primitive Iroquois or Algonkin deities, there are a few which are actual traditions, though much confused and distorted, of incidents that really occurred. Among these is the story told by Clark, of the marvelous bird by which Hiawatha's only daughter was destroyed. Longfellow has avoided all reference to this preposterous tale; but to Mr. Clark, if we may judge from the fullness and solemnity with which he has recorded it, it appeared very impressive. [1] According to his narrative, when the great convention assembled at the summons of Hiawatha, to form the league of the Five Nations, he came to it in company with his darling and only daughter, a girl of twelve. Suddenly a loud rushing sound was heard. A dark spot appeared in the sky. Hiawatha warned his daughter to be prepared for the coming doom from the Great Spirit, and she meekly bowed in resignation. The dark spot, rapidly descending, became an immense bird, which, with long and pointed beak and wide-extended wings, swept down upon the beautiful girl, and crushed her to atoms. Many other incidents are added, and we are told, what we might well believe, that the hero's grief for the loss so suddenly and frightfully inflicted upon him was intense and long protracted.

That a story related with so much particularity should be utterly without foundation did not appear probable. It seemed not unlikely that a daughter of Hiawatha might have been killed at some public meeting, either accidentally or purposely, and possibly by an Indian belonging to one of the bird clans, the Snipe, the Heron, or the Crane. But further inquiry showed that even this conjecture involved more of what may be styled mythology than the simple facts called for. The Onondaga chiefs on the Canadian Reserve, when asked if they had heard anything about a strange bird causing the death of Hiawatha's daughter, replied at once that the event was well known. As they related it, the occurrence became natural and

---

[1] "Onondaga," Vol. I, p. 25.

intelligible. It formed, indeed, a not unimportant link in the chain of events which led to the establishment of the confederacy. The catastrophe, for such it truly was, took place not at the great assembly which met for the formation of the league, but at one of the Onondaga councils which were convened prior to that meeting, and before Hiawatha had fled to the Caniengas. The council was held in an open plain, encircled by a forest, near which temporary lodges had been erected for the Councillors and their attendants. Hiawatha was present, accompanied by his daughter, the last surviving member of his family. She was married, but still lived with her father, after the custom of the people; for the wife did not join her husband in his own home until she had borne him a child. The discussions had lasted through the day, and at nightfall the people retired to their lodges. Hiawatha's daughter had been out, probably with other women, into the adjacent woods, to gather their light fuel of dry sticks for cooking. She was great with child, and moved slowly, with her faggot, across the sward. An evil eye was upon her. Suddenly the loud voice of Atotarho was heard, shouting that a strange bird was in the air, and bidding one of his best archers shoot it. The archer shot, and the bird fell. A sudden rush took place from all quarters toward it, and in the rush Hiawatha's daughter was thrown down and trampled to death. No one could prove that Atotarho had planned this terrible blow at his great adversary, but no one doubted it. Hiawatha's grief was profound; but it was then, according to the tradition of the Canadian Onondagas,--when the last tie of kindred which bound him to his own people was broken,--that the idea occurred to him of seeking aid among the eastern nations. [1]

Clark's informants also told him much about a snow-white canoe in which Hiawatha-or, rather, Ta-oun-ya-wa-tha-made his first appearance to human eyes. In this canoe the demigod was seen on Lake Ontario, approaching the

---

[1] This account of the events which immediately preceded Hiawatha's flight differs somewhat from the narrative which I received from the New York Onondagas, as recorded in the Introduction (p. 22). The difference, however, is not important; and possibly, if it had occurred to me to inquire of these latter informants about the incident of the bird, I might have heard from them particulars which would have brought the two versions of the story still nearer to accord. The notable fact is that the reports of a tradition preserved for four hundred years, in two divisions of a broken tribe, which have been widely separated for more than a century, should agree so closely in all important particulars. Such concurrence of different chroniclers in the main narrative of an event, with some diversity in the details, is usually regarded as the best evidence of the truth of the history.

shore at Oswego. In it he ascended the river and its various branches, removing all obstructions, and destroying all enemies, natural and preternatural. And when his work was completed by the establishment of the League, the hero, in his human form of Hiawatha, seated himself in this canoe, and ascended in it to heaven, amid "the sweetest melody of celestial music."

The nucleus and probable origin of this singular story is perhaps to be found in the simple fact that Hiawatha, after his flight from the Onondagas, made his appearance among the Caniengas a solitary voyager, in a canoe, in which he had floated down the Mohawk river. The canoes of the Caniengas were usually made of elm-bark, the birch not being common in their country. If Hiawatha, as is not unlikely, had found or constructed a small canoe of birch-bark on the upper waters of the stream, and used it for his voyage to the Canienga town, it might naturally attract some attention. The great celebrity and high position which he soon attained, and the important work which he accomplished, would cause the people who adopted him as a chief to look back upon all the circumstances of his first arrival among them with special interest. That the canoe was preserved till his death, and that he was buried in it, amid funeral wails and mournful songs from a vast multitude, such as had never before lamented a chief of the Kanonsionni, may be deemed probable enough; and in these or some similar events we may look for the origin of this beautiful myth, which reappears, with such striking effect, in the closing scene of Longfellow's poem.

THE IROQUOIS TOWNS

THE list of towns comprised in the text contains twenty-three names. Of this number only eight or nine resemble names which have been in use since the Five Nations were known to the whites; and even of this small number it is not certain that all, or indeed any, were in these more recent times applied to their original localities. My friend, General John S. Clark, of Auburn, N. Y., who has made a special study of the positions of the Indian tribes and villages, and whose notes on this subject illustrate the excellent work of Dr. Hawley on the early history of the Cayuga nation, [1] has favored me, in a recent letter, with the following brief but valuable summary of what is known in regard to the Iroquois towns:--

"When the Mohawks were first known, they occupied three principal towns on the south side of the Mohawk river, between Canajoharie and Schoharie creeks. The most eastern was that of the "Turtles" (or Tortoise clan), and was usually designated as such, and by the Dutch as the Lower or First Castle. The Middle or Second Castle was commonly termed the village of the "Bears;" while the Third or Upper Castle was generally called Teonnondoge or Tionnontogen, a name apparently having reference to the 'two mountains' near which the original town stood. After these towns were destroyed by the French, in 1666, their people removed to the north side of the river,--those of the lower town retreating a few miles up the stream to the rapids; and then for a hundred years this was generally known as Caughnawaga (Kahnawake) "At the Rapids." The Middle or Second Castle was called Gandagaro in 1670, Kanagiro in 1744, etc. The third appears to have retained its old name in all positions.

"When the Oneidas were first known they occupied a position on the headwaters of the Oneida inlet, and afterward gradually drew northward toward the lake. Their great town was usually called by the name of the tribe, as Onneiot, Onoyut, etc. One site, occupied about 1700, was called and known generally as Kanowaroghare, said to signify 'a head on a pole.'

---

[1] Early Chapters of Cayuga History: By Charles Hawley, D. D., President of the Cayuga Historical Society.

"The Onondagas, first known in 1615, occupied several sites, from a point south of the east end of Oneida lake, where they were when first known, to the Onondaga valley; but in all cases the chief town, when named, was called Onondaga, from the name of the tribe. Their great village in the Onondaga valley, according to Zeisberger, was known in 1750 as Tagochsanagecht, but this was a form derived from the name of the Onondagas as used in council. In all ages this chief town, wherever located, had other minor towns within from two to five miles, but they are rarely named. The great town was also divided into districts, one for each clan, each of which must have been known by the clan name, but this is seldom referred to. This rule held good also in all the large towns. A 'Bear village' was not occupied exclusively by members of the Bear clan; but these predominated and exercised authority.

"The Cayugas in 1656 occupied three villages,--Onnontare, on a hill near the Canandaigua river,--Thiohero, near the foot of Cayuga lake ('By the Marsh,' or, 'Where the Rushes are'),--and a third, which generally took the name of the tribe, Cayuga, but was occasionally divided into three districts, like the other large towns.

"The Senecas, when visited by the Jesuits, occupied two great towns, and several minor villages. The eastern of the two towns, near Victor, was called Gandougarae. The western, on Honeoye creek, nearly always, in all localities, took the name of the stream, which signifies 'bending.' It is said that when the League was first formed, it was agreed that the two great Seneca towns should be called by the names of two principal sachems; but I am unable to find that this was carried out in practice. In La Hontan's narrative of the De Nonville expedition, the great western town was separated into two parts, Thegaronhies and Danoncaritowi, which were the names of two important chiefs; while De Nonville's and other accounts describe it as Totiakton, 'at the bend.' This discrepancy, however, is found in all cases where the several towns are mentioned, as it was quite common to speak of them by the name of the principal chief. Thus, Cayuga in 1750 was called Tagayu, from Togahayu, the well-known chief sachem; Onondaga was called Canasatago's town, etc."

The frequent changes in the positions and names of Indian towns, thus well explained and exemplified, will account for the fact that so few of the ancient names in the list which the tenacious memories of the record-keepers retained have comedown in actual use to modern times. The well-known landmark of the Oneida stone seems to have preserved the name of the town,--Onenyute, "the projecting rock,"--from which the nation derived its usual designation. Deserokenh, or, as the Jesuit missionaries wrote it, Techiroguen, was situated near the outlet of the Oneida lake, at the point where the great northern trail crossed this outlet. A village of some importance is likely to have been always found at or near that locality. The same may be said of Deyuhhero, or Tiohero, where the main trail which united all the cantons crossed the river outlet of Lake Cayuga.

In other cases, though the identity of names is clear, that of the localities is more doubtful. The Kaneghsadakeh of the list, the "Hill-side town," may be the Kanasadaga of the Senecas; but, as General Clark remarks, the name might have been applied to any town on the side of a mountain. In like manner Deyughsweken (or Deyohsweken), which is said to mean "flowing out," may have been the town from which the Oswego river took its name, or a town at the mouth of any other river; and Deyaokenh, "the Forks," may have been Tioga, or any other village at the junction of two streams. Jonondese ("it is a high hill") is perhaps the same name as Onontare, which in Charlevoix's map appears as Onnontatacet; [1] but the name may well have been a common one. A few other apparent coincidences might be pointed out; but of most of the towns in the list we can only say that no trace remains in name or known locality, and that in some cases even the meaning of the names has ceased to be remembered. General Clark sums up his conclusions on this point in the following words: "They appear to belong to a remote--I may say a very remote--age, and not to be referred to any particular known localities; and this, as it appears to me, is more to the credit of the manuscript as an archaic work."

---

[1] See "Early Chapters of Cayuga History," p. 4.

THE PRE-ARYAN RACE IN EUROPE AND AMERICA

[The following is the concluding portion of an essay on "Indian Migrations, as evidenced by Language," which was read at the Montreal meeting of the American Association for the Advancement of Science, in August, 1882, and published in the "American Antiquarian" for January and April, 1883. As the views set forth in this extract have a bearing on the subjects discussed in the present work, the author takes the opportunity of reproducing them here for the consideration of its readers.]

It will be noticed that the evidence of language, and to some extent that of tradition, leads to the conclusion that the course of migration of the Indian tribes has been from the Atlantic coast westward and southward. The Huron-Iroquois tribes had their pristine seat on the lower St. Lawrence. The traditions of the Algonkins seem to point to Hudson's Bay and the coast of Labrador. The Dakota stock had its oldest branch east of the Alleghenies, and possibly (if the Catawba nation shall be proved to be of that stock), on the Carolina coast. Philologists are well aware that there is nothing in the language of the American Indians to favor the conjecture (for it is nothing else) which derives the race from eastern Asia. But in western Europe one community is known to exist, speaking a language which in its general structure manifests a near likeness to the Indian tongues. Alone of all the races of the old continent the Basques or Euskarians of northern Spain and southwestern France have a speech of that highly complex and polysynthetic character which distinguishes the American languages. There is not, indeed, any such positive similarity, in words or grammar, as would prove a direct affiliation. The likeness is merely in the general cast and mould of speech; but this likeness is so marked as to have awakened much attention. If the scholars who have noticed it had been aware of the facts now adduced with regard to the course of migration on this continent, they would probably have been led to the conclusion that this similarity in the type of speech was an evidence of the unity of race. There seems reason to believe that Europe--at least in its southern and western portions--was occupied in early times by a race having many of the characteristics, physical and mental, of the American aborigines. The evidences which lead to this conclusion are well set forth in Dr. Dawson's recent work on "Fossil

Man." Of this early European people, by some called the Iberian race, who were ultimately overwhelmed by the Aryan emigrants from central Asia, the Basques are the only survivors that have retained their original language; but all the nations of southern Europe, commencing with the Greeks, show in their physical and mental traits a large intermixture of this aboriginal race. As we advance westward, the evidence of this infusion becomes stronger, until in the Celts of France and of the British Islands it gives the predominant cast to the character of the people. [1]

If the early population of Europe were really similar to that of America, then we may infer that it was composed of many tribes, scattered in loose bands over the country, and speaking languages widely and sometimes radically different, but all of a polysynthetic structure. They were a bold, proud, adventurous people, good hunters and good sailors. In the latter respect they were wholly unlike the primitive Aryans, who, as was natural in a pastoral people of inland origin, have always had in the east a terror of the ocean, and in Europe were, within historic times, the clumsiest and least venturous of navigators. If communities resembling the Iroquois and the Caribs once inhabited the British islands and the western coasts of the adjacent continent, we may be sure that their fleets of large canoes, such as have been exhumed from the peat-deposits and ancient river-beds of Ireland, Scotland, and France, swarmed along all the shores and estuaries of that region. Accident or adventure may easily have carried some of them across the Atlantic, not merely once, but in many successive emigrations from different parts of western Europe. The distance is less than that which the canoes of the Polynesians were accustomed to traverse. The derivation of the American population from this source presents no serious improbability whatever. [2]

---

[1] "The Basque may then be the sole surviving relic and witness of an aboriginal western European population, dispossessed by the intrusive Indo-European tribes. It stands entirely alone, no kindred having yet been found for it in any part of the world. It is of an exaggeratedly agglutinative type, incorporating into its verb a variety of relations which are almost everywhere else expressed by an independent word."--The Basque forms a suitable stepping-stone from which to enter the peculiar linguistic domain of the New World, since there is no other dialect of the Old World which so much resembles in structure the American languages." Professor Whitney, in "The Life and Growth of Language," p. 258.

[2] The distance from Ireland to Newfoundland is only sixteen hundred miles. The distance from the Sandwich Islands to Tahiti (whence the natives of the former group affirm that their ancestors came) is twenty-two hundred miles. The distance

On the theory which seems thus rendered probable, that the early Europeans were of the same race as the Indians of America, we are able to account for certain characteristics of the modern nations of Europe, which would otherwise present to the student of anthropology a perplexing problem. The Aryans of Asia, ancient and modern, as we know them in the Hindoos, the Persians, and the Armenians, with the evidence afforded by their history, their literature and their present condition, have always been utterly devoid of the sentiment of political rights. The love of freedom is a feeling of which they seem incapable. To humble themselves before some superior power--deity, king, or brahmin--seems to be with them a natural and overpowering inclination. Next to this feeling is the love of contemplation and of abstract reasoning. A dreamy life of worship and thought is the highest felicity of the Asiatic Aryan. On the other hand, if the ancient Europeans were what the Basques and the American Indians are now, they were a people imbued with the strongest possible sense of personal independence, and, resulting from that, a passion for political freedom. They were also a shrewd, practical, observant people, with little taste for abstract reasoning.

It is easy to see that from a mingling of two races of such opposite dispositions, a people of mixed character would be formed, very similar to that which has existed in Europe since the advent of the Aryan emigrants. In eastern Europe, among the Greeks and Sclavonians, where the Iberian element would be weakest, the Aryan characteristics of reverence and contemplation would be most apparent. As we advance westward, among the Latin and Teutonic populations, the sense of political rights, the taste for adventure, and the observing, practical tendency, would--be more and more manifest; until at length, among the western Celts, as among the American Indians, the love of freedom would become exalted to an almost morbid distrust of all governing authority.

---

from the former islands to the Marquesas group, the nearest inhabited land, is seventeen hundred miles. The canoes of the Sandwich Islands (as we are assured by Ellis, in his p. 189 "Polynesian Researches,") "seldom exceed fifty feet in length." In the river-beds of France, ancient canoes have been found exceeding forty feet in length. One was more than forty-five feet long, and nearly four feet deep. Seethe particulars in Figuier's "Primitive Man," Appleton's edit., p. 177. See also Prof. D. Wilson's "Prehistoric Man," 2d edit., p. 102, for a full discussion of this question, with instances of long canoe voyages.

If this theory is correct, the nations of modern Europe have derived those traits of character and those institutions which have given them their present headship of power and civilization among the peoples of the globe, not from their Aryan forefathers, but mainly from this other portion of their ancestry, belonging to the earlier population which the Aryans overcame and absorbed. That this primitive population was tolerably numerous is evident from the fact that the Aryans, particularly of the Latin, Teutonic, and Celtic nations, lost in absorbing it many vocal elements and many grammatical inflections of their speech. They gained, at the same time, the self-respect, the love of liberty, and the capacity for self-government, which were unknown to them in their Asiatic home. Knowing that these characteristics have always marked the American race, we need not be surprised when modern researches demonstrate the fact that many of our Indian communities have had political systems embodying some of the most valuable principles of popular government. We shall no longer feel inclined to question the truth of the conclusion which has been announced by Carli, Draper, and other philosophic investigators, who affirm that the Spaniards, in their conquest of Mexico, Yucatan, and Peru, destroyed a better form of society than that which they established in its place. The intellectual but servile Aryans will cease to attract the undue admiration which they have received for qualities not their own; and we shall look with a new interest on the remnant of the Indian race, as possibly representing this nobler type of man, whose inextinguishable love of freedom has evoked the idea of political rights, and has created those institutions of regulated self-government by which genuine civilization and progress are assured to the world.

CANIENGA GLOSSARY

THE following Glossary comprises all the words of the Canienga text. The meanings of these words are given as they were received from the interpreters. For most of them these definitions are confirmed by the dictionaries of Bruyas and Cuoq. Some of the words, which are either archaic forms or peculiar to the Council ceremonies, are not found in those dictionaries; and in a few instances the precise purport of these words must be considered doubtful. In some cases, also, the force of a grammatical inflection or of an affix may not have been correctly ascertained; but it is believed that the vocabulary will be found, in general, sufficiently accurate to be of service to the student who may desire to acquire some knowledge of the Canienga speech.

When the words of John Buck's copy differ in orthography from those of the Johnson MS., the former are added in brackets. Words cited from the dictionary of Bruyas are distinguished by the letter B; those from the lexicon of M. Cuoq by C.

A.

Aerengh [orenh], far. Heren, ahiren, B., far; heren, aheren, C., far away.

Aesahhahiyenenhon [ahesahhahiyenennyonhon], if thou hadst fallen (or perished) by the way. Aha, oha, ohaha, road, path; gaienneñon, B., to fall.

Aesayatyenenghdon [ahesayatyenendon], thou mightest have been destroyed. Gaienneñon, B., to fall; gaiennenton, to cause to fall. Aesaiatienenton is in the perf. subj. passive.

Aghsonh, scarcely, hardly, while.

Ai (excl.), hail! oh!

Aihaigh (excl.), hail! ah! oh! More commonly pronounced haihai.

Akare, until.

Akayongh [akayon], ancient. Akaion, C., old, ancient, antique.

Akonikonghkahdeh, they are suffering. Onikonhra, mind, and oga'te, B., raw., i.e., having a sore mind.

Akotthaghyonnighshon, one who belongs to the Wolf clan. See Sathaghyonnighshon.

Akwah, indeed, truly, very, yea.

Akwekon, all.

Are, again, sometimes.

Ayakawen, one would have said. En, B., to say(perf. subj.).

Ayakaweron, one would have thought. Eron, B., to think, to wish.

Ayakotyerenhon, one would be startled, surprised. From katyeren, to wonder, be startled.

Ayawenhenstokenghske [ayawenhensthokenske], may it be true. Eñon, iaweñnon, B.,--iawens, C., to happen; togenske, B., tokenske, C., it is true. "May it happen to be true!"

Ayuyenkwaroghthake [ayoyenkwarodake], there might have been tobacco smoke (apparent). Oienkwa, C., tobacco; gar8t, B., to smoke (ppf. subj.).

D.

Da-edewenhheye [dahedewenheyeh], we may, all die. Genheion, genheie, B., to die (subj. mood).

Daghsatkaghthoghseronne [dasatkahthoseronne], thou mightest keep seeing. See Tesatkaghthoghserontye. Tasatkahthoscronne (as the word would be spelt in modern orthography) appears to be the aorist subjunctive of atkahthos, to see, in the cislocative and frequentative forms.

Daondayakottondeke, that they may hear. Athonde, to hear.

Deghniwenniyu, joint ruler; lit., they two are masters. See Rawenniyo.

Deghsewenninekenne, thou mayest speak. See Entyewenninekenneh.

Dendewatenonghweradon, in our mutual greetings. See Dewadadenonweronh.

Denghsatkaghdonnyonheke [densatkatonhnyonsekeh], thou wilt be looking about thee. Atkahthos, to see.

Denighroghkwayen [dehnihrohkwayen], let us two smoke. Garok8a, B., une pipe, touche de petun. It is conjectured that the name Iroquois, i. e. "Tobacco-people," may have been derived from this word. See Appendix, Note A.

Dentidewaghneghdoten, we will replace the pine-tree. Ohnehta, pine. Oten, as a suffix (according to M. Cuoq), "serves to express the condition, the manner, the kind, the nature of a thing."

Denyakokwatonghsaeke [tenyakokwennhendonghsaeke], he will be dying. Desakk8atonch, Onon. Dict., I am dying; kanon8enton, B., sick.

Denyontadenakarondako, they shall take off his horns. Onakara, horn.

Desahahishonne, thou art coming troubled.

Desakaghserentonyonne, thou comest weeping. Gagasera, B., tear.

Desanyatokenh, in thy throat. Oniata, C., throat, neck.

Desawennawenrate, thy voice coming over. From owenna, C., ga8enda or ga8eniza, B., voice, speech, word, and a8enron, B., to pass over. The cislocative prefix de (te) gives the sense of "hither."

Deskenonghweronne [deskenonweronne], I come again to greet and thank. Kannonh8eron, B., to salute any one; kannonh8eronton, to salute or thank by, or for, anything. See ante, page 149, for an analysis of this word.

Detkanoron [detkanorons], all but, almost. From kanoron, costly, important, difficult.

Dewadadenonweronh [dewadatenonweron], mutual greeting. Kannonh8eron, B., to salute any one.

Dewaghsadayenhah, in the shade. Asatagon, B., in secret; asatakon, C., in the dark.

Deyakodarakeh, the two clans. Ohtara, C., tribe, band. (Dual or duplicative form.)

Deyakonakarondon, wearing horns, i. e., being chiefs. Onnagara, B., horn; kannagaront, having horns; gannagaronni, B., être considérable.

Deyughnyonkwarakda [deyohnyonkwaraktah], at the wood's edge; near the thicket. Onniong8ar, B., thorn-bush, bramble; akta, C., beside, near to. The word applies to the line of bushes usually found on the border between the forest and a clearing. With the cislocative prefix de it means "on this side of the thicket."

Deyughsihharaonh [deyohsiharaonh], there is a stoppage. Gasiharon, B., to stop up, to close.

Deyunennyatenyon, hostile agencies, opposing forces. Gannenniani, B., to surprise or defeat a band; gannennaton, ib., to seek to destroy.

Deyunhonghdoyenghdonh [deyonhonghdoyendonh], mourning wampum. This word appears to be composed of three of Bruyas' radices, viz.,--gaionni, 'wampum belt (collier de porcelaine),--gannonton, to throw wampum for the dead,--and gaienton, to strike, whence skaienton, to return the like, to strike back, and gaientatonton, to give satisfaction for any one wounded or killed; and the meaning will be "wampum given as a satisfaction or consolation for a death."

Dhatkonkoghdaghkwanyon [thatkonkohdakwanyon], in going through. Ongóon, B., to penetrate, to pass through; atongotahkon, B., the place through which one passes.

Doghkara [dohkara], only a few. Tohkara, C., only occasionally, a few, a small number of.

Doka, if, perhaps, either, or. Toka, C., or, if, I don't know.

Donghwenghratstanyonne [donwenratstanyonne], coming over. A8enron, B., to pass over.

E.

Eghdejisewayadoreghdonh [eghdetsisewayadorehdonh], this ye considered, ye deliberated about this. Kaiato`reton, B., to examine, to think, to deliberate about anything.

Eghdeshotiyadoreghton they again considered. (See the preceding word.)

Eghnikatarakeghne [eghnikadarakene], such were the clans. Ehni--, C., for ethoni, there are, so, it is thus that; ohtara, clan, band.

Eghnikonh, thus, in this way.

Eghnonweh, thither, yonder.

Eghtenyontatitenranyon, they will condole with one another, or, there will be mutual condolence. Gentenron, B., kitenre, C., to pity any one. Atatitenron, B., to deplore one's misery.

Eghyendewasenghte, we will let it fall. Aseñon, B., to fall; asenhton, ib., to cause to fall.

Eghyesaotonnihsen, this was his uncle. See yeshodonnyh.

Endewaghneghdotako, we will pull up a pine tree. From onehta, pine, and gatak8an, gatako, to draw out, B., sub voce At.

Enghsitskodake, thou wilt be resting, thou wilt remain. Gentskòte, B., to be in any place.

Entyewenninekenneh, the words which will be said. From Kawenna, word (q. v.) and en, B., to say.

Enjerennokden (or enyerennokden), they will finish the song; or, the hymn will be finished. Karenna, song, hymn; okte, B., the end; to finish.

Enjeyewendane [enjewendane], they will be comforted. Ga8eienthon, B., to be calm. (This word should probably be written enjeyeweyendane.)

Enjondatenikonghketsko, they will comfort, lit., will raise the mind. Onikonhra, mind, spirit, temper, and gagetsk8an, B., to raise up.

Enjondentyonko. See Enyonghdentionko.

Enjonkwakaronny, it will cause us trouble. Gagaronnion, B., to do harm to any one, to cause him some loss.

Enjonkwanekheren, we shall suffer a loss. Wakenekheren, C., not to know, not to recognize (i.e., we shall cease to see some one).

Enskat, one, once.

Entkaghwadasehhon, will be vexed, excited. Gah8atase, B., to twist, turn round.

Enwadon, it will be allowed. Watons, fut. enwaton, C., to be possible, feasible, allowed.

Enwadonghwenjadethare, will make a hole through the ground. See Onwentsia.

Enyairon, they will say, one will say. From en, B., fut. egiron, to say.

Enyakaonkodaghkwe [enyakaonkohdakwe], they shall have passed. Ongóon, B., to penetrate, pass through; ongotanni, to cause to penetrate, etc.

Enyakodenghte, they (or one) will be miserable. Genthentéon, B., to be deserving of pity.

Enyakodokenghse [enyakodokenseh], they (or one) will discover. Gatogeñon, gatogens, B., to know.

Enyakohetsde [enyakohetste], he (or one) will go on. Kohetstha, C., to pass beyond.

Enyakonewarontye, they (or one) will be surprised. Ganne8aron, B., to surprise.

Enyeharako, they will carry it. Gaha, B., to carry off

Enyeken, they will see. Gagen, B., to see.

Enyenikonghkwendarake, they will be mourning. Onikonhra (q. v.) and gag8entaron, stretched on the ground (i.e., the mind dejected).

Enyerennokden. See Enjerennokden.

Enyerighwanendon [enyerihwanondon], they will ask (or, will wonder). From karihwa (q. v.) and gannendon, B., to wonder, or annonton, to seek. Garihwanonton, B., to ask the news.

Enyerighwawetharho, the business will be closed. Karihwa (q. v.) and otarhon, B., to grasp; kotarhos, C., to grasp, to stop by grasping.

Enyonderennoden, they will sing it thus. Karenna, q. v. and --oten, C., which "serves to express the condition, manner, kind, or nature of a thing."

Enyonghdentyonko, he will walk to and fro. Atention, B., to go away.

Enyononghsaniratston, it will strengthen the house. Kanonsa, house, and ganniraton, B., to strengthen.

Enyontsdaren, they will weep. Katstaha, C., to weep, to shed tears.

Enyontyerenjiok, they will be startled. From katyeren, to wonder, to be surprised.

Enyurighwadatye [enyorihwadatye], it will continue: the affair will go on. From kariwa (q. v.) as a verb, in the progressive form and future tense.

Etho, thus, so.

Ethone, then.

Ethononweh, thither.

H.

Hasekenh, because. Aseken, C., for, because.

Henskerighwatonte [enskerighwatonte], I will frustrate their purposes. From karihwa (q. v.) and aton`ton, B., to cause to lose, to mislead.

Henyondatsjistayenhaghse [henyondatstsistayenhase], they will hold a council, lit., they will make a council fire. From katsista, fire; gatsistaien, B., to hold council, to light the council fire.

Hone, also. See Ony.

I.

Ie [iih], I.

Iese [ise], thou, ye.

Iesewengh, ye have said. En, B., to say.

Issy [hissih], yonder, there. Isi, C., there.

J.

Jadadeken, thy brother (or brothers). Tsiatatekenha, C., ye two are brothers.

Jadakweniyosaon (or jatagweniyosaon), thou wert the ruler, or, ye were the rulers. See Jadakweniyu.

Jadakweniyu, thou art the ruler, or, ye are the rulers. See note to Sec. 28, ante, p. 152.

The Iroquois Book of Rites

Jatatawhak, father and son, lit., son of each other. Gahawak, B., to have for child (reciprocal form).

Jathondek (or jatthontek), listen! hearken thou. Imperative sing. of kathontats, C., athontaton, B., to hear.

Jatthontenyonk, keep listening! continue to hear! The frequentative form of jatthontek.

Ji [tsi], that, that which, wherein. See Jini.

Jidenghnonhon [jidennon], as, like as. Tennon, C., and also, but.

Jinayawenhon, the consequences, the results, lit. what would happen. Eñon, B.,--iawens, C., to happen.

Jinesadawen [tsinesadawen]. See Jinisadawen.

Jini [tsini], that which, such, so, so much.

Jinihotiyerenh, what they did. From Jini (q. v.) and --kierha, --wakieren, C., to act, do, say. This verb is always preceded by some particle, such as kenni (see how), tsini (that which) and the like.

Jinikawennakeh, these the words. See Jini and kawenna.

Jinisayadawen [tsinesayadawenh], that which has befallen you. Eñon, B., to happen; gaiata8eñon, to happen to some one.

Jiniyuneghrakwah [tsiniyohnerakwa], this solemn event. Gonneragoon, B., to wonder; jonnerag8at, that is wonderful. See yuneghrakwah.

Jinonweh [tsinonweh], thither, whereto.

Jiratighrotonghkwakwe [tsiradirohtonhkwakwe], where they, used to smoke. Gar8t, B., to smoke; otonkwa, C., flame. "Where they lighted their pipes."

Jisanakdade [tsisanakdate], from thy seat. See Kanakta.

Jiyudakenrokde [tsiodakenrokde], by the fireplace, near the ashes. Akenra, ashes; okte, end, edge.

Jiyathondek, listen! hearken! Imperative dual of kathontats, I hear. See jathondek.

Jodenaghstahhere, they made additions to a house; they added a frame. Gannasta, B., poles for making a house; onasta, C., a framework; kaheren, B. to be upon.

Joskawayendon, there is again wilderness, waste ground. Gaienthon, B., to have fields.

K.

Kadon, I say, I speak. Igatonk (sub voce En), B., I say; katon, G, to say.

Kady [kadi], therefore, then. Kati, C., then, consequently.

Kadykenh, because. See Katykenh.

Kaghnekonyon, floods. From ohneka, water, in the frequentative form. Gannegonnion, B., there is much water.

Kaghyaton, it is written. Kiatons, C., to write. M. Cuoq says: "the perfect participle takes an h: kahiaton, written, it is written," Gaiatare, B., to paint.

Kajatthondek, listen! See Jathondek.

Kakeghrondakwe, they were collected; were assembled. Gageron, B., to be together, or, to put things or persons somewhere.

Kanaghsdajikowah [kanastatsikowah], great framework, great building. From kanasta, frame, and kowa, great.

Kanakaryonniha, on a pole. Gannagare, B., pole, long stick.

Kanakdakwenniyukeh, on the principal seat. From kanakta (q. v.), and atakwenniio, C., principal.

Kanakdiyuhake, the place (or seat) may be good. From kanakta, place, seat, and --iyu, good (subjunctive mood).

Kanakta, mat,--hence couch, bed, seat, place.

Kaneka, where, somewhere.

Kanekhere, I believe, I suppose; surely, certainly. Probably from eron, igere, B., to think, or suppose.

Kanhonghdakdeh [kanonhdakdeh], by the wall, or side of the house. Onnhonta, wall of house, of a cabin; akte, beside, athwart.

Kanikonrashon, the minds, a plural form of Onikonhra, (q. v.)

Kanikonrakeh, in mind. See Onikonhra.

Kanonghsakdatye [kanonsakdatye], outside the house. Kanonsakta, near the house; from Kanonsa, house, and akta, near, beside. The progressive affix tye gives the meaning of "passing near the house."

Kanonghsakonshon [kanonsakonshon], in the house.

Kanonsa, house.

Kanoron, important, valuable, serious, difficult, painful, afflicting.

Karenna, song, hymn, chant.

Karighwakayonh, in ancient times. From Karihwa (q. v.), and akaion, old. See Orighwakayongh.

Karighwatehkwenh [karihwahtehkonh], this word, which the interpreters rendered simply ceremony, probably means "the fire-kindling act," from Karihwa (q. v.), and atehken, or atekha (ategen, atexa, B.), to burn.

Karihwa or karighwa (garih8a, B., kariwa, oriwa, C.), thing, affair, business, action, news, word. This word, in its root-form of rihwa (riwa) or riho, enters largely into compounds having reference to business, law, office, news, belief, and the like.

Karonta, tree, log, trunk, post.

Kathonghnonweh. [kathounonweh], I fail, I lose my way. Atoñon, B., to lose one's self, to go astray.

Kathonghdeh, away, out of sight. Atonhton, B. (sub voce atoñon), to cause to lose, to mislead.

Katykenh [kadikenh], how then? Kati, C., then (done); ken, interrogative particle.

Kawenna (ga8enda, ga8enna, B.; owenna, C.), word, voice, language, speech.

Kayanerenh, peace, goodness, justice, law, league. Wakianere, ioianere, C., to be good, right, proper (i.e., noble); roianer, he is a chief. Kaianerensera, law, government, rule, decree, ordinance. See ante, p. 33.

Kayanerenghkowa, great peace, great law, the great league. Kayanerenh (q. v.) and kowa, great.

Kehaghshonha, kehhasaonhah, recent, lately.

Ken (for kento) here.

Kendenyethirentyonnite, here we will place them. See Kenderentyonnih.

Kenderentyonnih, this is lying here. Probably from Ga renton, B., to hang down, and ionni, to be extended or laid out.

Kendonsayedane (?) returning here, (qu., pausing here). Gasaien, B., to be slow; gasaiatanne, to make slow.

Kenenyondatyadawenghdate, one shall be murdered here. A8enthon, B., to kill; Katawenthos, C., to kill many people, to massacre.

Kenhendewaghnatatsherodarho, we will attach a pouch. Gannata, B., little bag; otarhon, to grasp.

Kenkaghnekonyon, here floods. See kaghnekonyon.

Kenkarenyakehrondonhah, being hidden here among logs. Gagarennion, B., to remove away; Karonta, tree, log.

Kenkine [kenki], thus, in this way.

Kenkisenh [kenhkense], thus, in this way.

Kenkontifaghsoton, here things lying in ambush.

Kenne, thus.

Kennikanaghsesha, small strings of wampum. Kenni--ha, C., small, kanahses, (?) a string of wampum.

Kensane, but, however.

Kentekaghronghwanyon [kondekahronwanyon], here obstacles. Ga`ronhon, B., to place (or to be) athwart.

Kentewaghsatayenha, here in the dark. Asatagon, C., in the darkness; asatagon, B., in secret.

Kenteyurhoton, here to this opening (or cleared space in a forest). Karha, forest.

Kenthoh (kento, C.), here.

Kenwaseraketotanese, here the uplifted hatchet, From ken, here, wasera (asera, osera), hatchet, and gaget8t, B., to be shown, to appear above.

Kenwedewayen, we place it here. From ken, here, and gaien, B., to put in any place.

Kenyoteranententenyonhah, there is a crevice here. From ken, here, and ateronnonte, B., having space, or showing light between two things not well joined.

Kenyutnyonkwaratonnyon, here many thorns. From ken, here, and onniong8ar, B., thorns, brambles. The word is in the frequentative form.

Konnerhonyon [konneronyon], they keep thinking. Eron, B., to think, to will. (Frequentative form.)

Konyennetaghkwert [konyennedaghkwen], my child, my offspring. From ennet, B., to hold an infant in one's bosom. "Goñyennetak8an, says the Canienga to the Oneida," B. Konyennetahkwen is properly a verb of the third conjugation, in the imperfect tense, and the 1:2 transition: "I nursed thee as a child." Here it is used idiomatically as a noun.

Kowa, kowane, great.

N.

Nadehhadihne, it was their number. See Natejonhne.

Nadekakaghneronnyonghkwe [nedekakanneronnyonkwe], it was commonly looked at. Kagannere, B., to see (frequentative form, imperfect tense).

Nai (exclam.), hail! oh! ah! (It is the exclamation ai or hai, with the particle ne prefixed.)

Nakonikonra, their mind. See Onikonhra.

Nakwah, (?) indeed. See Akwah.

Natehotiyadoreghtonh, they decided on. Kajato`reton, B., to examine, think, deliberate about anything.

Natejonhe, it was your number; this was the size of your class. Teionihes, C., large, wide; "ken ok nateionhes, not larger than that."

Nayakoghstonde [nayakostonde], by reason of, the pretext being. Gastonton, B., to make a pretext of anything.

Nayawenh, it may be. Eñon, yaweñon, B., --iawens, C., to happen. See Nenyawenne.

Nayeghnyasakenradake, (?) having a white neck. Onniasa, B., neck; gagenrat, B., white.

Ne, the, this, that, who, which (rel.). A demonstrative and relative particle, variously used, but always giving a certain emphasis to the word which it precedes.

Nedens, either, or.

Nekenne (or ne kenh ne), thus.

Nene, the, this, that, these, those, etc. (an emphatic reduplication of ne).

Nenyakoranne, they will keep on, persist, go so far as. Gara`on, garanne, B., to find any one; keras, kerane, C., to approach any one, to come to him.

Nenyawenne, it may be; it will happen; it shall be done. Future of Naya-wenh, q. v.

Nenyerighwanendon, they will inquire. See Enyerighwanendon.

Neok, nok, and, also. (Contracted from ne and ok.)

Neony [neoni], also. See Ne and Oni.

Niateweghniserakeh, every day. From niate, each, every, and wehnisera (or wennisera) day, with the locative participle ke.

Nitthatirighwayerathaghwe [nithariwayerathakwe], they used to do the work. From karihwa, business, and gaieren, B., to do. (Imperfect tense.)

Nityakwenonontonh, they search, inquire, pry into. Annonton, gannenton, B., to seek, search, interrogate.

Niuterenhhatye (?) it was startling. From katyeren, to wonder, to be startled.

Niwa, extent, size, number.

Niyakoghswathah, they are mischievous, troublesome. Gas8aton, B., être méchant.

Niyawehkowa [niawenhkowa], great thanks. Niawen, C., thanks; kowa, great.

Niyawennonh, it happened. See Nayawenh.

Niyenhhenwe [niyenhhenwe], in the future. --nenwe relates to the future, C.

Niyieskahhaghs, being borne. Gaha, B., to carry away.

Niyonsakahhawe, he is carried. Gahawi, B., to bring.

Noghnaken, hereafter, afterwards, in later times. See Oghnaken.

Nonkenh, it may be. Eñon, B., to happen.

Nonkwaderesera, our grandchildren. See Saderesera.

Nonwa, now.

Nyare, while, previously. Niare, C., beforehand.

O.

Oghentonh, in the first place, foremost, firstly. Gahenton, B., to go first; ohenton, C., before, foremost, formerly.

Oghnaken [onaken], afterwards. Ohnaken, C., behind, backwards, afterwards.

Oghniyawenhonh, what has happened. From ohni, C., what? and iawens, to happen.

Oghnonekenh, dismayed (?) Kannonhiannion, B., to fear, to be alarmed.

Oghseronnih [onhseronni], together. Oseronni, C., together.

Oghsonteraghkowa [aghsonderahkowah], disease, pestilence.

Ohhendonh; see Oghentonh.

Ok, and, also, indeed.

Okaghserakonh [okaserakonh], in tears. Gagasera, B., tears.

Okaghsery [okaseri], tears. Okaseri, C., tear, from Okahra, eye, and keri, liquid.

Onakara, horn.

Onekwenghdarihenh, in crimson (i.e., in blood). Onig8entara, B., red; onnig8ensa, blood.

Onenh [onen]. Now; at last; finally.

Onghteh [onhteh], perhaps, probably.

Onghwa, now, at present. Onwa, C., now. (Same as Nonwa.)

Onghwajok, presently.

Onghwenjakonh [onwenjakon], into the earth. See Onwentsia.

Onidatkon, deadly.

Onikonhra, mind, character, disposition, thought, opinion, sentiment. Gandigon`ra, B., esprit, pensée.

Onkwaghsotshera [onkwasotsera], our forefathers. The root is sot, meaning grandparent. Rak`sotha, C., my grandfather; ak`sotha, my grandmother; onkwa, our; sera, the "crement," generalizing the word.

Onkwaghsotsherashonhkenha, our deceased forefathers. See Onkwaghsotshera. Shon (son) is the plural suffix; kenha, deceased, "the late" (the French feu).

Onok, and, and then. See Ony, Ok and Neok.

Onokna, and then.

Onwa, now. See Onghwa.

Onwentsia, earth, land, field, ground.

Ony [oni], also. See Neony.

Orighokonha, few words. From karihwa (q. v.), and okonha, an affix indicating a restricted plural.

Orighwakayongh [oriwakayon], in ancient times. See Karihwa and Akayongh.

Orighwakwekonh [oriwakwekon], all business, all matters, all the rules. See Karihwa and Akwekon.

Owenna. See Kawenna.

Oya [oyah], another, another thing.

Oyata (or oyada), body, person, some one, self; Oiata, C., body, person; gaiata, B., living thing.

Oyeukondonh, men, warriors (obsolete).

R.

Radiyats. See Ratiyats.

Rakowanenh, he is chief (lit. he is a great one). From kowanen, to be great; root, kowa, great.

Ranyaghdenghshon [ranyadenhshon], he is of the Tortoise clan. Keniahten, C., to be of the Tortoise band.

Ratikowanenghskwe, they were great. 3d person, plural, imperfect of kowanen, to be great. See Rakowanenh.

Ratiyanarenyon [radiyanaronnyon], their many footmarks, or traces. Gaianna, B., oiana, C., track, trace (frequentative form). Gaiannaranyon, B., there are many tracks.

Ratiyats, they call it. 3d person, plural, of Gaiason, B., to name, to call.

Raweghniseronnyh [rawenniseronni], he appoints (lit. makes) the day. From weghnisera, day, and konnis, C., to make.

Rawenniyo [rawenniyoh], God (lit. he is a master). Keweniio, C., to be master. See Appendix, note B.

Raxhottahyh, my forefathers. Rak`sotha, C., my grandfather.

Roghskenrakeghdekowah, he is a war-chief Oskenra, C., war; roskenra-kehte, warrior; kowa, great.

Rodighskenrakeghdethaghkwe [rodiskenrakedetahkwe], they were warriors. 3d pers. pl. imperfect of roskenrakehte, he is a warrior.

Rokhawah, his son. Gaha8ak, B., to have for child; niha8ak, my child.

Rokwahhokowah, he is the great wolf Okwaho, wolf; kowa, great.

Ronarasehsen, they are cousins. See Yeshonarase.

Ronatennossendonghkwe [rondennoshentonhkwe], they used to meet (lit., to fraternize). 3d pers. pl. imperfect of atennossen, to be brother and sister.

Ronenh, they said. En, B.. to say (used only in the preterite).

Roneronh, they thought. Eron, B., to think.

Ronkeghsotah, my forefathers. See Onkwaghsotshera and Raxhottahyh.

Roskerewake, he is of the Bear clan. Akskerewake, C., to be of the band of the Bear.

Rotirighwison, they made the rule, they decided. See Karihwa. Garih8ison, B., to finish a matter, to conclude.

S.

Saderesera, thy grandchildren. Atere, grandchild; sera, the crement, generalizing the word. See Onkwaghsotshera.

Sahondakon, in thy ears. Ahonta, B., ear.

Sanekenh, although, yet, nevertheless.

Sanekherenhonh, thou art losing.

Sanheghtyensera, thy women, thy womankind. Gannhetien, B., woman; sera, the generalizing affix. See Saderesera.

Sanikonra, thy mind. See Onikonhra.

Sathaghyonnishon, thou art of the Wolf clan. Tahionni, one of the Wolf clan.

Senirighwisaanonghkwe, ye two were the founders. See Sewarighwisaanonghkwe.

Seniyatagweniyohkwe, ye two were the principals. See Jadakweniyu; the affix kwe indicates the past tense.

Sewarighwisaanonghkwe [sewarihwisahanonkwe], ye established, ye were the founders. From karihwa, q. v., and gason, B., to finish, to consummate. Garihwisaani, B., to accomplish a work, to complete a business.

Sewatarighwakhaonghkwe, ye were combined in the work, ye joined heartily in the business. From karihwa, (q. v.) and gagaon, B., to find good; gatih8agáon, B., to like the affair.

Seweghne [sewenghne], ye said. En, B., to say.

Seweghniserathagh, for a time, lit., for a day. See Weghniserade.

Seweryenghskwe, ye who were comrades. (?) Probably from Oeri, C., friend, comrade,--here a verb in the imperfect tense.

Shehaweh [shehawa], thy child, or children. See Rohhawah.

Shekonh, yet, still. Sekon, C., still, moreover.

Shihonadewiraratye, they with their children (lit., they kept on producing young ones). From yodewirare, a fowl hatching.

Skaendayendon, again a waste place. Oyente, B., woods; gaienthon, to have fields. (Reiterative form).

Skarenhesekowah, a lofty tree; lit., a great tree-top. From garenha, B., tree-top, ese (suffix) long, high, and kowa, great.

Skennen, well, easily, peacefully, pleasantly.

Skennenji, quite well, very peacefully, safely. From skennen and tsi, C. an augmentative affix.

T.

Tehhodidarakeh, the two clans. See Tekadarakehne.

Tehotyatakarorenh, acting in two capacities (lit., a person divided). From oiata, person, and tioren, B., to split.

Tekadarakehne, there were two clans, or, of the two clans. From otara or katara, clan or totem (in the reduplicate form and past tense).

Tesatkaghthoghserontye [tesatkahthohserontye], thou sawest in coming. Katkathos, C., to see, look. The cislocative, frequentative, and progressive forms are all combined in this expressive word--"you kept seeing as you came."

Thadenyedane (?), he will stand. Gataon, B., to raise himself upright.

Thadenseghsatkaghthonnyonheke [thadensehsatkatonnyonheke], thou mayest look about thee. Katkathos, C., to look (frequentative form, subjunctive mood).

Thadetyatroghkwanekenh, let us two smoke together, From garok8a, B., kahrokwa, C., a pipe. Bruyas gives the derivative form t8atrok8annegen, but does not explain it; it evidently means, "let us (pl.) smoke together."

Thensadondeke, thou wilt hear. Athonte, athontaton, B., kathontats, C., to hear, obey, consent.

Thienkahhawe, will carry. Gahawi, B., to bring.

Thisayatatirhehon [thisayadadirhehon], thou arrivest.

Thisennekwakenry, thou art sitting in blood. Ganneg8e, B., blood, and gagenrion, to roll, to wallow.

Thiwakwekonh [ohtihwakwekonh], all around.

Thiyaensayeken, they will see it again. Gagen, B., to see.

Thiyenjidewatyenghsaeke [thienjidewatyenseke], we shall have reached home; lit., we shall have taken a seat. Atient, atien, B., to sit down.

Tsini; see Jini.

Tsisaronkatah, thy hearing. Arongen, B., to hear, to listen; arongaton, B., to hear by anything.

Tyewenninekenne, he will speak some words. See Entyewenninekenneh.

Tyeyadakeron, bodies are lying. Oyata, body; gageron, B., to be in any place.

Tyoghnawatenghjihonh [dyonawaghdehtsihonh], a swift current. Ohnawa, C., current, swift stream of water; ganna8tetan, B., swift river; tsihon, an augmentative suffix,--"exceedingly swift."

W.

Waahkwadewayendonh, taking care, carefully. Ate8eyenton, B., to take care, to do well.

Waghontenhnonterontye, or Wahhondennonterontye, they were as brothers thenceforth. Atennonteron, to be brothers. The word is in the aorist indicative, 3d pers. pl., progressive form (indicated by the termination tye).

Wahhoronghyaronnon, he put away the clouds. From aronhia, sky, heaven, cloud.

Wakarighwakyone [wakarihwakayonne], it has become old. See Karighwakayonh.

Wakatyerenkowa, I was greatly surprised. From katyeren, to wonder, or be startled, and kowa, greatly.

Wakonnyh [wakonnikih], woman, womankind. (Obsolete.)

Wakwenekwenghdarokwanyon, we have washed off the bloodstains. Garag8entara, B., blood, and garag8an, to take away, or garag8egan, to efface.

Wakwennyonkoghde, I have stopped for you (as tears). Probably from ganniong, B., the nose; kannionkon, to bleed from the nose, i.e., flowing from the nose.

Watidewennakarondonyon, we have put the horns on him (i.e., made him a chief). Onnagara, B., horn; gannagaronni, B., être considérable.

Watyakwasiharako, we have removed the obstruction, we have unstopped. Gasiharong8an, B., to unstop (desboucher).

Watyonkwentendane, we have become wretched, or poor. Genthentéon, B., to be worthy of compassion.

Wedeweyennendane (see under Wete--).

Wedewennakeraghdanyon (see under Wete--).

Weghniserade [wenniserade], to-day. Ennisera, B., day; nonwa wenniserate, C., to-day.

Wetewayennendane, we have finished. Gaweyennentáon, B., to rest, to cease from working.

Wetewennakeraghdanyon [wedewennakeratanyon], we have made the signs, we have gone through the ceremonies. Ganneraton, B., "se servir de règle."

Y.

Yadayakonakarondatye, he may be going with horns. From onakara, horn (progressive form, subjunctive mood).

Yadehninhohhanonghne, they two guarded the door, they two were the doorkeepers. Gannhoha, B., door; gannonna, to guard.

Yaghdekakoghsonde [yaghdegagonhsonde], invisible, (lit., without face); from yahte, not, and kakonhsa (okonsa) face.

Yaghnonwenh, never. Iah-nonwenton, C., never. From Iah (yah) not, and nonwa or onwa, now.

Yakwenronh, we say. En, B., to say.

Yatehhotinhohhataghkwen, they were together at the doorway (i.e., they were the doorkeepers). Gannhoha, B., door; atakon, B. (sub voce At), "ce dans quoi il y a."

Yatenkarighwentaseron, to finish the business. From karihwa (q. v.) and awentas, to finish.

Yejisewahhawitonh, ye have taken it with you. Gaha8i, B., to bring; gaha8iton, to take away.

Yejisewatkonseraghkwanyon, ye have it as a pillow. Esakonserak8a, B., thou wilt use as a pillow.

Yejisewayadkeron [yetsisewayatakeron], ye are laid together. Gageron, B., to be together, to place together.

Yejodenaghstahhere, they added a frame. See Jodennaghstahhere.

Yendewanaghsende, we will drop (or let fall) into it. Aseñon (?), B., to fall; asenhton, to cause to fall.

Yenjontahidah, they will follow. Gataxon, gataxi, B., to run.

Yenyontatenontshine, they are to be led by the hand. Probably from gannonna, B., to keep, and atsi, comrade.

Yenyontatideron, they shall be placed. Genteron, B., to put any animate thing in any place.

Yeshodonnyh, or Yeshotonnyh, his uncle (properly, "his father's younger brother"); also, as pl., his uncles. `Atonni, C., a relative on the father's side. The prefix yes, in which the signs of the translocative and reiterative forms are combined, gives the sense of "the next younger (uncle) but one."

Yeshohawah, or Yeshohawak, his next younger child but one. See Rohhawah, and Yeshodonnyh.

Yeshonadadekenah, or Yeshondadekenah, they are brothers. Rontatekenha, C., they are brothers together. This word is made up of the prefix ye, the sign of the translocative form; s, of the reiterative form (see Yeshodonnyh); ron or rona, the plural pronoun (they); tate, the sign of the reciprocal form; ken, younger brother; and ha, an affectionate diminutive affix, generally added to words expressing relationship.

Yeshonarase, his second cousin (lit., they are cousins). Arase, cousin. See Yeshodonnyh.

Yeshonaraseshen, he was their cousin. See Yeshonarase.

Yeshotiriwayen, they have again referred the business. From karihwa, q. v.

Yetsisewanenyadanyon, ye are in your graves. Perhaps from onenya, stone,--ye are under the stones.

Yetsisewanonwadaryon, ye have taken your intellects (lit., brains) with you. Ononwara, C., brain, head.

Yetsisewennitskagwanion, ye have placed it under you. Ennitsk8are, B., to be seated on anything.

Yondonghs, it is called; they call it. Katon, C., to say.

Yonkwakaronny, they are wasting, or injuring, us. Gagaronnion, B., to do harm to any one; to cause him some loss.

Yonkwanikonghtaghkwenne [yonkwennikondakwenne], we depended on them.

Yontkwatkennison, we are assembled. Atkennison, B., to be assembled.

Yotdakarahon [yotdarahon], things falling on one. Ga`ráon, B., to fall upon.

Yoyanere, it is good, it is well. From the root yaner, noble. See Kayanerenh.

Yuneghrakwah, solemn event. See Jiniyuneghrakwah.

Read these similar books for free at forgottenbooks.org:

Myths of the Cherokee

Iroquoian Cosmology

Jicarilla Apache Texts

Apu Ollantay

Seneca Indian Myths

The Popol Vuh

The Cherokee Ball Play

The Book of the People: Popol Vuh

The Book of Chilam Balam of Chumayel

Many Swans, Sun Myth of the North American Indians

Read or order online at:

www.forgottenbooks.org
or
www.amazon.com

Printed in Germany by
Amazon Distribution
GmbH, Leipzig